W0051277

Cambridge Lower Secondary

Complete English

Series Editor: Dean Roberts
Annabel Charles, Alan Jenkins,
Mark Pedroz, Tony Parkinson

Second Edition

7

WORKBOOK

OXFORD
UNIVERSITY PRESS

Great Clarendon Street, Oxford, OX2 6DP, United Kingdom

Oxford University Press is a department of the University of Oxford. It furthers the University's objective of excellence in research, scholarship, and education by publishing worldwide. Oxford is a registered trade mark of Oxford University Press in the UK and in certain other countries

© Oxford University Press 2021

The moral rights of the authors have been asserted

First published in 2021

All rights reserved. No part of this publication may be reproduced, stored in a retrieval system, or transmitted, in any form or by any means, without the prior permission in writing of Oxford University Press, or as expressly permitted by law, by licence or under terms agreed with the appropriate reprographics rights organization. Enquiries concerning reproduction outside the scope of the above should be sent to the Rights Department, Oxford University Press, at the address above.

You must not circulate this work in any other form and you must impose this same condition on any acquirer

British Library Cataloguing in Publication Data
Data available

978-1-38-201925-5

10 9 8 7 6 5

Paper used in the production of this book is a natural, recyclable product made from wood grown in sustainable forests. The manufacturing process conforms to the environmental regulations of the country of origin.

Printed in India by Multivista Global Pvt. Ltd.

Acknowledgements
We are grateful for permission to reprint the following copyright material:

Extract from It's All About the Bike: The Pursuit of Happiness on Two Wheels (Penguin Particular, 2010). Copyright © Robert Penn 2010.

Cover illustration: Charles Harker/Getty Images.

Photos: p68(l): Everett Collection/Shutterstock; p68(r): iStock.com/ duncan1890.

Artwork by Integra Software Services and Six Red Marbles.

Although we have made every effort to trace and contact all copyright holders before publication this has not been possible in all cases. If notified, the publisher will rectify any errors or omissions at the earliest opportunity.

This Workbook refers to the Cambridge Lower Secondary English (0861) Syllabus published by Cambridge Assessment International Education.

This work has been developed independently from and is not endorsed by or otherwise connected with Cambridge Assessment International Education.

Table of contents

The power of suggestion

Writers of suspense deliberately keep their readers guessing for most of the storyline. This is because the power of suggestion is a very useful tool for authors. Example:

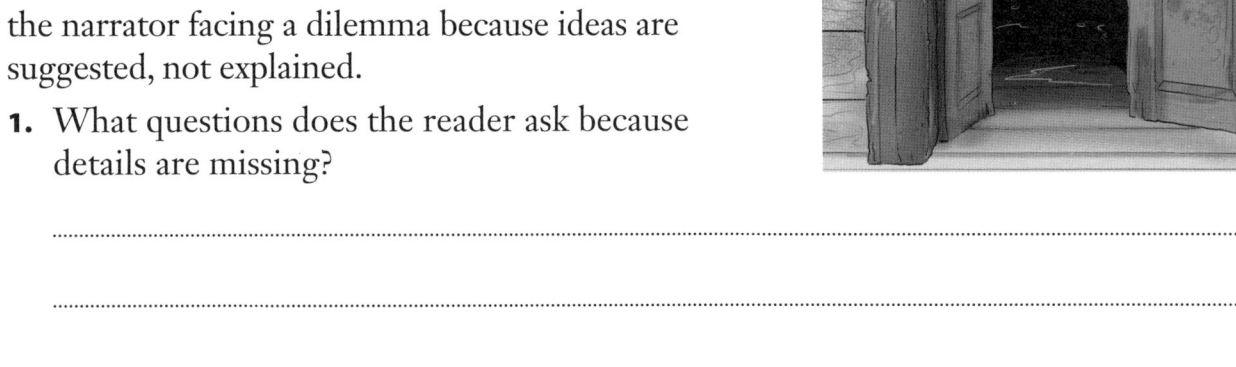

I stood by the barred gate of the ramshackle house. Should I go in? Should I run? What would become of me if I entered? Finding the courage, I approached the door. As I did, it opened slowly. . .

This extract sets the scene for a sinister mood, with the narrator facing a dilemma because ideas are suggested, not explained.

1. What questions does the reader ask because details are missing?

   ....

   ....

   ....

2. How does the lack of details make this extract full of suspense?

   ....

   ....

3. Write a paragraph where a character is faced with a serious dilemma. Build suspense by suggestion and by omitting details.

   ....

   ....

   ....

   ....

   ....

   ....

Using effective verbs

Using the most suitable verbs can create a vivid image in a reader's mind and help to build atmosphere.

1. Depending on the image the writer wanted to create, the way a yeti walks could make it seem threatening, friendly or humorous.

   Place these walk-related verbs in the most suitable box.

   pranced   exploded   flew   trundled
   danced   strolled   loped   lolloped
   shuffled   lurked   shambled   hulked
   waddled   strode

threatening	**friendly**	**humorous**

2. Choose one yeti and use verbs to describe its first meeting with humans.

   Happy yeti

   Angry yeti

   Hurt yeti

   Shy yeti

   ....

   ....

   ....

   ....

Simple and compound sentences

Remember

A simple sentence has one main clause and can stand alone.

A compound sentence has two main clauses, normally separated by the use of a conjunction. A conjunction is a joining word.

1. Put an 'S' or a 'C' next to each of the following to show whether it is a simple or compound sentence.

   a Sara grew up watching horror films.

   b All of the movies at the festival were good but *Frankenstein* was Tariq's favourite.

   c Simple sentences have one main clause but compound sentences have two or more main clauses.

2. Change these simple sentences into compound sentences.

   a The movie was really good. I am glad I went to see it.

   ....

   b I really like suspense in stories. I don't like horror.

   ....

   c I am pleased to have bought tickets for the concert. I was afraid they would sell out before I reached the venue.

   ....

   ....

3. Using a conjunction, pair these main clauses into five compound sentences, making a paragraph about a scary theme park ride.

It is taller than the Statue of Liberty.

Verruckt stands at over 50 metres high.

There are no safety restraints to hold you in.

There are 264 stairs to climb to enter the ride.

Verruckt is a water slide.

You sit in a plastic tube shaped like a boat.

Tests showed riders were not secure.

It isn't a rollercoaster at all.

The opening of the ride was delayed.

Accessing Verruckt is far from easy.

Advisory adverbs

1. Complete the following news report, using the health and safety adverbs.

securely

understandably

clearly   delicately

SAFETY FIRST!

attentively   prudently

alertly

Today, officials .... doled out the first batch of approved air canisters to people in District 41. The canisters had all passed quality controls and were packaged .... They were each covered in bright red linings bearing the words 'Open .... to avoid leakage'. A cordon of security guards watched the proceedings .... to ensure that order was maintained. After all the canisters were distributed, the people listened .... while a senior official read out the operating instructions. One woman, who was .... concerned, questioned the officials about what to do if her canister proved to be faulty. The official replied .... , informing her to report the issue to the health and safety committee at the District 41 offices.

2. a Write five adverbs you would see on a fire escape sign or an earthquake evacuation sign.

b Then write an evacuation drill using your five adverbs. Write just one paragraph.

Exit

....

....

....

....

....

Complex sentences

1. Use the Venn diagram to match up six complex sentences. Write the new sentences in the space below.

Remember

A complex sentence contains one main (independent) clause and one or more subordinate (dependent) clauses, linked by a subordinating conjunction.

Spiders are arachnids
Some spiders are venomous
Some spiders are nocturnal
Always check for spiders
Spiders have eight legs
People fear spiders

although
even though
whereas
which
because
before

insects have six legs.
most aren't a threat to
humans. they're quick and
silent. was a Greek word
originally. others hunt in the
day. putting on your shoes.

2. Use these subordinating conjunctions to make five complex sentences: *after*   *whenever*   *if*   *as*   *until*

Hyphenated compounds

1. Put hyphens in the right places in the following words.

   a longsighted ....

   b shortterm ....

   c reelect ....

   d shortlived ....

   e substandard ....

2. All of the words below begin with a single capital letter, followed by a hyphen and then the rest of the word, as in *S-bend* (a pipe used in plumbing).

Draw lines to match each letter to its word. Some letters can be matched to more than one word.

T-	neck
X-	boat
	turn
V-	shirt
	junction
U-	ray

> **Remember**
>
> Hyphens connect two or more words to form one idea. These become hyphenated compounds.
>
> Hyphens can also be used where there is ambiguity.

3. What happens to the meaning of the following phrases if the hyphens are removed?

   a *short-story* writer

....

....

....

   b the old book was *re-bound*

....

....

....

   c *re-cover* that damaged book please

....

....

....

Writing suspense

Creating suspense involves keeping the reader guessing about what is going to happen next.

1. Write what will happen next in these scenarios.

   a She couldn't hold on much longer. She could feel the numbness in her fingers gradually spreading...

     ....

     ....

   b Just a few more metres. At last he felt safe. But then...

     ....

     ....

   c Why, oh why hadn't they followed their friend's advice? Now it was too late. In the shadows something stirred.

     ....

     ....

2. Creating suspense also involves time pressure. Write an ending for each scenario.

   a With the monster stirring, he only had a few minutes to ....

   b Once the detonator was triggered, Aysha knew she ....

   c Just four minutes was all she had to ....

3. Creating suspense is about the main character facing a challenging dilemma. Think of a dilemma for each of these characters to solve.

   a Simone standing on a platform waiting for a train to arrive

     ....

     ....

   b The scientist trying to decide whether to let his creature loose

     ....

     ....

Spine-chilling suspense quiz

1. Write two effective verbs to describe how a sea monster might move.

   ....

2. What is the main difference between a simple sentence and a compound sentence?

   ....

   ....

3. Underline the four adverbs in this passage:

   Sitting quietly watching the lazily setting sun, I couldn't believe how I'd escaped so amazingly unscathed from my trip to see the monkeys. I breathed calmly for the first time in hours.

4. What kind of sentence is this? Explain your answer.

   She had to help her friend because she knew snakes frightened him.

   ....

   ....

   ....

5. What are subordinating conjunctions? Identify the conjunction here.

   Whenever I travel, I take at least two suspense novels to read.

   ....

   ....

6. Why is this a good beginning to a horror suspense story?

   I had been hiding for hours. Too scared to move; too confused to know where to go next. Just wishing it would stop chasing me.

   ....

   ....

   ....

Turn off the news! It's trouble, trouble, trouble!

Baby talks at four months

Young inventor shows off his work

GIRL WINS ART AWARD

Summer sunshine has arrived

New theme park opens

Cure for disease found

TV show steals the airwaves

Some people say there's too much bad news in the newspapers. They say that, although we need to know some things that are bad, it would be better if we were also told about some good things, to provide a balance.

Imagine you are an editor-in-chief and you have told your staff to produce tomorrow's newspaper with nothing but good news in it.

1. Choose four stories you would publish and write a headline for each of them.

    a ....

    b ....

    c ....

    d ....

2. Choose one of your headlines and write your report to go with it.

....

....

....

....

....

....

A strange occurrence

Midnight Mystery at New Theme Park

Residents were awakened in the early hours of yesterday by a low rumbling noise that grew into creaks and groans, before ear-splitting fairground music started up. Five minutes later, the sky was lit up by multi-coloured flashing lights and some dark figures were seen running about.

"It was madness," said one sleepless lady. "Everyone was up at their windows or out in the street. We feared there was some sort of disturbance or riot."

The noise came from a new theme park and fairground, due to be opened next month. Residents said that if they had known about this level of deafening cacophony they would have campaigned against it. The owner was not available for comment and the police have launched an investigation into what happened.

1. The headline says 'Midnight Mystery ...'. Do you think the noise started exactly at midnight? Explain your answer.

   ....

   ....

2. In your own words, explain how the disturbance increased.

   ....

   ....

3. Use the context given in the article to suggest what *cacophony* means.

   ....

4. Why do you think the police were called?

   ....

   ....

5. Write down a possible explanation for what happened.

   ....

   ....

6. Write the beginning of the newspaper article that followed up this story, published the next day.

Direct and indirect speech

1. Correct this passage of direct speech by putting in all the punctuation and capital letters.

   Remember to use apostrophes for contractions and speech marks for when you start and finish the words that someone says.

   we are going to learn all about mice said señora Elvira

   ugh i dont like mice said maria because they wriggle

   they actually make good pets said the teacher and they are very clean

   ive heard that you can eat mice said fredo

   you can smiled señora Elvira but not many people do

   they look cute she went on they have pointed

   noses and small rounded ears rather like you fredo

2. Now change the direct speech into indirect speech. Start like this:

   Señora Elvira said that the class was going to learn about mice.
   Maria made a disgusted noise and said that. . .

   ....

   ....

   ....

   ....

   ....

   ....

   ....

   ....

   ....

Make your case!

1. Think of three things that you really don't like and would like to complain about. You might complain about things you have to wear, rules you have to obey or TV programmes you don't like.

- ....
  ....
- ....
  ....
- ....
  ....

2. Choose one of these three topics, and write down three points you could use to make your case. Write two or three sentences on each. You will have to think about how to begin and how to end your speech. Write down your ideas in the space below.

Begin: ....

Point 1: ....

....

....

Point 2: ....

....

....

Point 3: ....

....

....

End: ....

....

Read through your notes, then put them down and start to write your speech.

Spelling adverbs – exceptions to the rule

Most adjectives can be changed into adverbs by adding –*ly*, but there are some exceptions, for example, the adjective *good*.

1. Correct the sentences below by deleting the incorrect adverbs.

    a   She revised good/goodly/well for her weekly test.

    b   He played more good/better/more well for Atletico Bueno.

    c. Sergio plays the drums worse/more badly/more rubbishly than Monica.

2. Complete these sentences.

    a   Anya can play the harp .... than Beatrice and performs in concerts.

    b   The team played .... after the half-time interval and the goalkeeper let in five goals.

3. Write three new sentences using *well*, *better* and *worse*.

    ....

    ....

    ....

    ....

    ....

    ....

    ....

    ....

Strange spellings of a simple sound

Say this verse aloud:

'What a strange thing about this word *sign* –

When you say it, the rhyme is with *shine*.'

In the newscast about the fire, the reporter said, "The fire shows no signs of dying down yet."

You can make several words by adding prefixes and suffixes to *sign*. *Sign* is a word that used to mean a mark.

1. The following words are hidden in the word search: assign, consign, design, ensign, resign, signpost.

   Find the six words and use a dictionary to check the meaning of any you do not know.

S	E	A	F	E	D	A	R
E	N	S	I	G	N	R	E
S	P	R	D	H	T	E	S
A	I	F	E	O	S	M	I
A	S	G	S	S	I	G	G
S	L	E	N	N	I	L	N
S	A	G	Y	P	A	D	G
I	W	K	E	Y	O	E	W
G	I	V	A	R	B	S	E
N	P	T	H	V	R	I	T
C	O	N	S	I	G	N	H

Remember

Prefixes are groups of letters added to the beginning of words to change the meaning of the original word. Suffixes have the same effect but are added to the end of words.

2. Match each of the six words to one of the clues below.

   a I point the way for you. ....

   b I am a flag. ....

   c I am a piece of artwork or a plan for a building. ....

   d I don't want to work here anymore; I shall ....

   e You hand it over or even get rid of it. ....

   f You give someone a task or appoint someone. ....

Expressing opinions in writing

You wrote a newspaper report on page 12. Imagine that it was published.

Now imagine that you are someone who has read the report. You decide to write an email or letter to the newspaper. In your letter, you say what you think about the events reported in the newspaper report.

You could:

- say how you agree with the report, and why
- use the report to set out your complaints and concerns
- add some of your own ideas and views to what was in the report – perhaps ideas for the future.

Remember to include an introduction, details of your ideas and an ending to your email or letter.

Dear Editor,

....

....

....

....

....

....

....

....

....

....

....

....

....

Yours faithfully,

Manic media quiz

1. a Using the prefixes and suffixes in the diagram, write down as many words as you can with the stem *tract*.

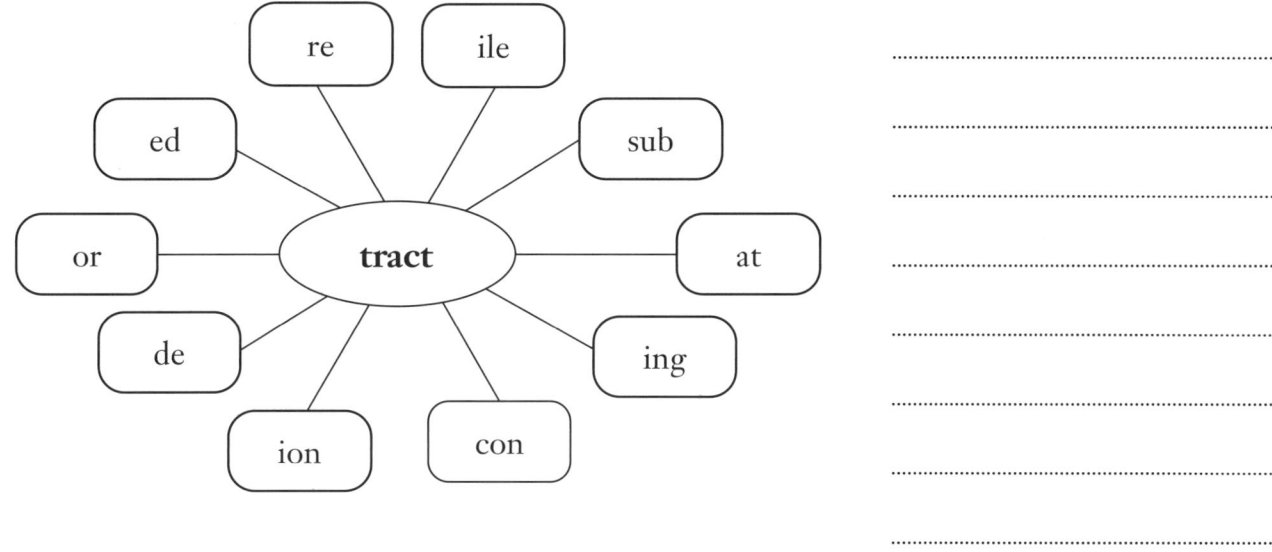

....

....

....

....

....

....

....

....

....

b Check the meanings of the words you have made using a dictionary.

2. Rewrite these headlines using alliteration.

a Luisa winning lots of money

....

....

b A sudden rush of water in the town of Fernandez

....

....

3. Turn this indirect speech into direct speech with the correct punctuation.

He told his father that he had decided to leave home. He needed to be independent.

....

....

....

3 Hazardous hobbies

Non-narrative poetry

1. Which of these statements best describes the qualities of
non-narrative poems? Tick the correct statements.

   Non-narrative poems:

   a always tell a story ⬭

   b don't have to rhyme ⬭

   c have one central idea ⬭

   d are always written in archaic language ⬭

   e can sometimes be funny ⬭

   f include kennings. ⬭

2. Using your responses to activity 1, write a definition for
non-narrative poetry.

   ....

   ....

3. Decide which of these are non-narrative poems by placing
a tick next to the title. Put a question mark by any that
could be non-narrative poems, even though you need more
information to be sure.

'How Brazil won the World Cup'

'The Art of Flying a Kite'

'My Team is Better than Yours'

'The Ballad of a Famous Cricketer'

'Slam Dunk'

'Javelin'

'The Day We Lost the Cup'

Extended metaphor

Hope is the thing with feathers

Hope is the thing with feathers
That perches in the soul
And sings the tune without the words
And never stops at all.

And sweetest in the gale is heard;
And sore must be the storm

That could abash the little bird
That kept so many warm

I've heard it in the chillest land
And on the strangest sea
Yet, never, in extremity
It asked a crumb of me.

Emily Dickinson

1. What is Emily Dickinson comparing hope to? ....

2. Underline the words in the poem that show the development of the metaphor comparing hope with something else.

3. **a** What do you think 'gale' and 'storm' in verse 2 represent?

   ....

   b What is the message in verse 2?

   ....

4. Suggest something else you could use as a metaphor for hope. ....

5. **a** What is being compared with what in each of these openings?

   i 'All the world's a stage, / And all the men and women merely players; /
   They have their exits and their entrances; / And one man in his time plays many parts'
   (William Shakespeare)

   ....

   ii 'The fog comes on little cat feet…' (Carl Sandburg)

   ....

   iii 'The sea is a hungry dog, / Giant and grey.' (James Reeves)

   ....

   b Choose one of these openings and write a poem that extends the idea of the metaphor.
   Try to create a rhythm or pattern in the length of your lines, your choice of words and
   the way you set your poem out on the page.

Imagery – similes and metaphors

Poets often use imagery to convey their message to readers. Creating an image in the mind of the reader helps because the human brain processes visual images more easily than written words.

Similes and metaphors are excellent tools to use when forming images. For example, if a poet wants to describe the power and precision of a tennis player's shot, it could be likened to a laser beam speeding towards its destination.

Remember

A simile is a way of comparing a person or a thing to something else.

A metaphor describes a person or a thing directly as something else.

1. Complete the following phrases to create a suitable image.

   a The angler caught a fish as big as a ....

   b The two boxers stood like .... facing each other in the ring.

   c The mountaineer climbed the peak like a .... climbing a

   ....

2. Create some similes or metaphors to describe:

   a a gymnast's athletic grace ....

   b a sprinter's power ....

   c an angry referee ....

   d a speedboat ....

Homonyms

Remember

Homographs are words that are spelled the same, but with different meanings.

Homophones are words that sound the same but have different meanings.

1. Write two sentences for each pair of homonyms to show their different meanings. (Hint: At least one word in each pair is related to sports and hobbies.)

a wind/wind

....

....

b cricket/cricket

....

....

c foul/fowl

....

....

2. The words on the cricket pitch have multiple meanings. For each word, write a sentence to demonstrate its non-cricket meaning. One has been given as an example. Continue on a separate sheet of paper if necessary.

Example: Use the scissors to cut out the shape.

....

....

....

....

....

....

....

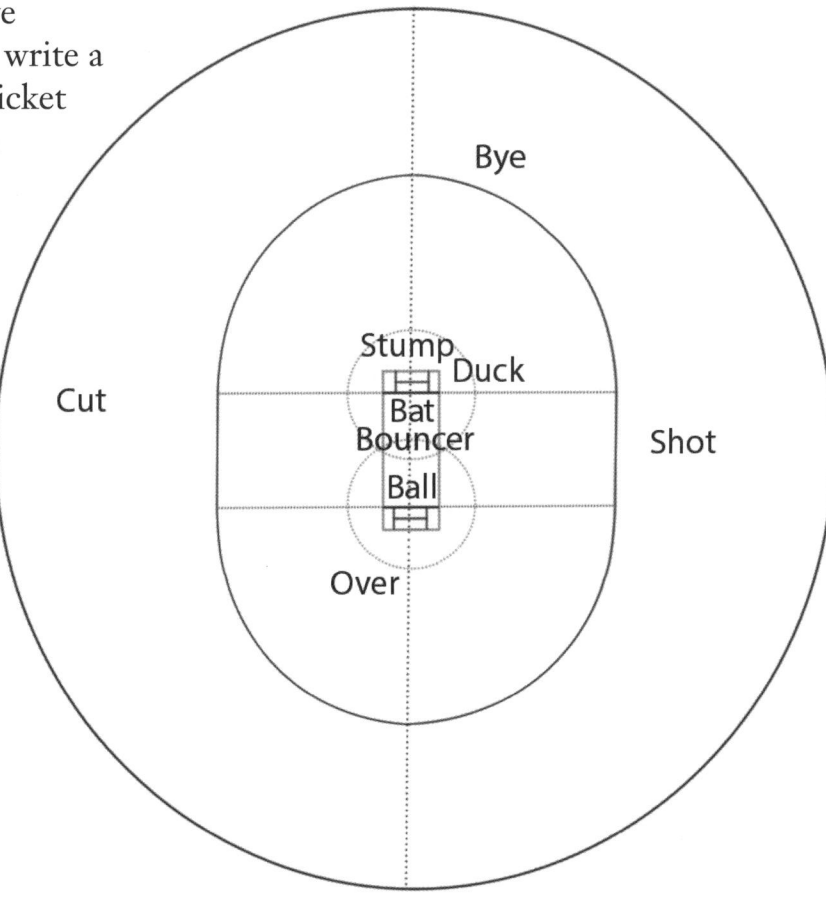

Alliteration

1. Underline examples of alliteration in this paragraph.

   Tennis players tend to be mentally tough and terrifically fit. Tortuous hours of practising tournament technique enable successful players to remain resolute even in the most taxing of situations. Ask any player what is the hardest part of their pre-tournament preparation and they will tell you it is the horrendously long hours of mind-bendingly boring, repetitive racket drills. They will also agree, however, that without this preparation they would not be the players they are.

2. One type of verse that uses alliteration is the tongue twister. This is a fun form of poetry that is meant to be spoken not read.

   a Try saying this phrase aloud very slowly and carefully.

   The souvenir shop sells soccer supporters' shirts, shorts and socks.

   b Now repeat this tongue twister five times as fast as you can. What happens? Suggest a reason for this.

   ....

   ....

   ....

3. Write your own tongue twister based on a sporting theme.

   ....

   ....

   ....

   ....

   ....

Remember

Alliteration occurs when two or more words close to each other start with the same letter or sound.

Analogies

1. Match the animal to the sportsperson. To match each pair think about the qualities each sportsperson must possess to be good at his or her sport. There are no right answers to this question, but you must be able to give a reason for the connections you make.

💡 **Remember**

An analogy is a comparison between two ideas that are alike.

boxer

gymnast

ice hockey player

marathon runner

sky diver

2. Write an analogy for each of the pairs in activity 1.

a ....

b ....

c ....

d ....

e ....

3. a Which analogy was the easiest to write? Explain your answer.

....

....

b Which was the most difficult? Explain your answer.

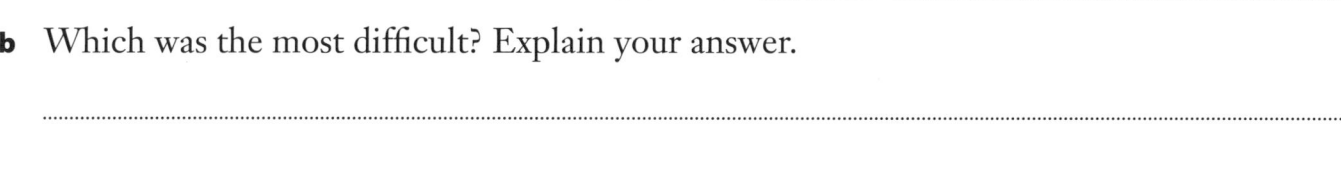

....

....

Spelling it out

An acrostic poem works by spelling out the subject of the poem vertically, using the first letter of the first word in each line. On the right is an acrostic poem about rugby.

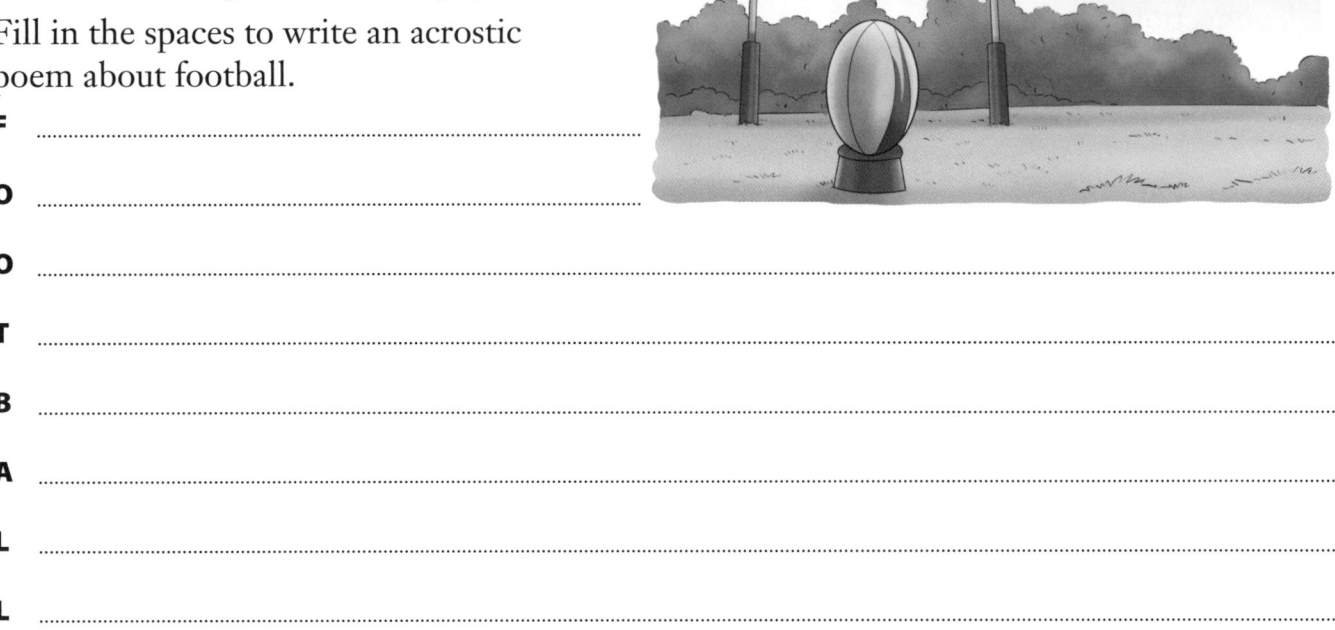

Rough
Unyielding
Gut-wrenching
Bone-crushing
You can't help but
    love playing it

1. Fill in the spaces to write an acrostic poem about football.

   F ....

   O ....

   O ....

   T ....

   B ....

   A ....

   L ....

   L ....

2. Write your own acrostic poem about a sport or hobby that interests you.

Hazardous hobbies quiz

1. Too many faces in the crowd, too many voices shouting out loud,

Willing me to miss, begging me to miss.

I score.

This is a complete poem about a footballer taking a penalty. Is this a narrative or non-narrative poem? Give a reason for your answer.

....

....

2. Write a metaphor.

....

3. The following paragraph contains eight homonyms (words with the same spelling or pronunciation but different meanings). Underline as many as you can find, using a dictionary to help if you are unsure.

A cricket umpire (referee) wears an amazing coat with pockets that seem bottomless. Into them go sticky tape, a pair of scissors, a plaster, hats, handkerchiefs and many other items. The space in there is mind-boggling.

4. What is the following an example of? Explain your answer.

The rugby player was surprisingly supple and stupendously strong.

....

....

5. What kind of literary technique is demonstrated here? Write another example of this.

As strong as a water buffalo, he was a successful weightlifter.

....

....

6. List the key features of a kenning.

....

....

Facts and opinions

Remember

Facts are statements that can be proven with evidence.

Opinions are views or beliefs. They are not necessarily based on facts.

1. Which one of these statements is a fact and which is an opinion? Write 'F' by the fact and 'O' by the opinion.

   a   I think vegetables are really tasty.

   b   Regular exercise and a healthy diet lessen the chance of heart disease.

2. Read this extract to decide which statements are facts and which are opinions. List the facts and opinions in the table below.

   > I eat lots of chocolate. Maybe too much, but it's so yummy and melts on your tongue. I prefer solid blocks of chocolate as they taste better. Chocolates with fillings inside are too sickly sweet. Two important ingredients in chocolate are milk and sugar. Sugar is used to sweeten the taste but is bad for your teeth and eating too much can cause tooth decay. I hate going to the dentist. The drill scares me even though my dentist is a really kind man. The next time I am tempted to eat a wonderful chocolate bar I'm going to think of going to the dentist to stop me eating the chocolate!

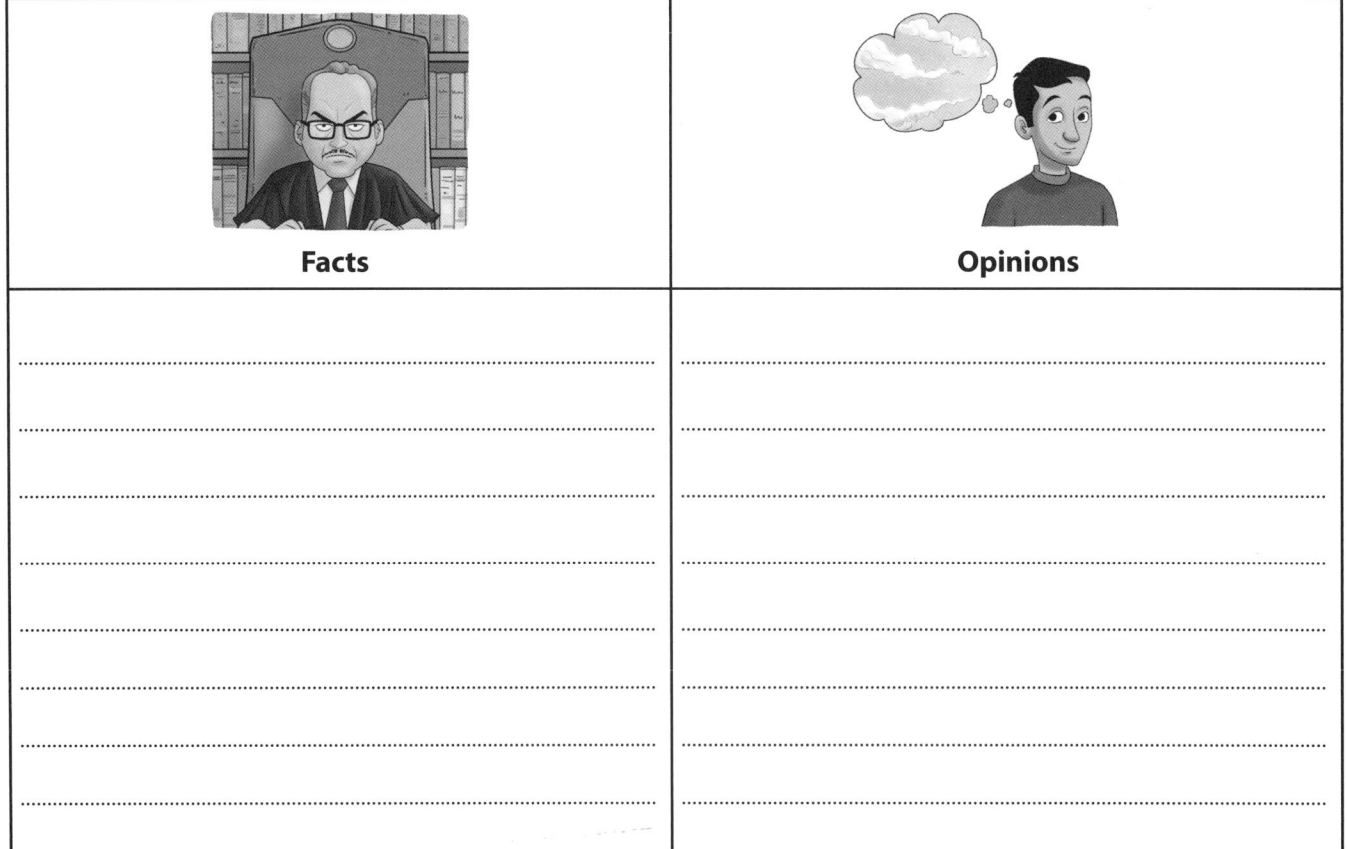

Facts	Opinions

Imperatives

Remember

Imperatives are commands. They are often used in writing to instruct or persuade the reader.

1. Find a suitable imperative for each of these statements. There are several possible answers.

   a ....! Road closed.

   b "... and you will hear what I am saying."

   c .... elephants crossing.

   d .... the ingredients well before pouring them into the pan.

   e "...! My oven is on fire!"

Do not eat the cake!

2. Write three imperatives for each scenario.

At school	By the roadside	Near water

3. Sara has to give a presentation to younger students about health and safety in the home. However, she is shy and doesn't know how to make her comments forceful enough. Write down five sentences using imperatives that will make Sara's presentation more effective.

   ....

   ....

   ....

   ....

   ....

   ....

   ....

Using the rule of three

1. Write a sentence using the rule of three to describe each food below. The first has been done for you.

   Your emphasis can either be positive or negative.

Remember

The rule of three is a technique used to stress the importance of certain points. Example:

Chill out! Stay calm! Relax!

Cabbage: Badly cooked cabbage is limp, slimy and disgusting.

Banana:

Chilli pepper:

Rice:

Sweet potato:

2. Write a short paragraph to describe the best features of your favourite food. Use as many examples of the rule of three as you can.

Being persuasive

When you are writing to persuade the reader to agree with
your ideas, you will show bias and use persuasive features.

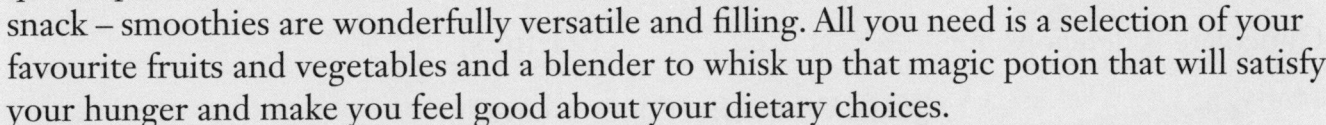

Not everything you read in health magazines will make you feel
better. Not every new health craze will guarantee a healthier you.
But this one will!

Smoothies are not just a craze; they're nutritious, yummily tasty and
amazingly easy to prepare. They're a fantastic way of adding the
recommended daily portions of fruit and vegetables to your diet.

It doesn't matter whether you drink them for breakfast, as a
quick option at lunchtime or for that secret midnight supper
snack – smoothies are wonderfully versatile and filling. All you need is a selection of your
favourite fruits and vegetables and a blender to whisk up that magic potion that will satisfy
your hunger and make you feel good about your dietary choices.

Nutritious, full of antioxidants and easy on your digestive system, smoothies are the perfect
answer to a hectic modern lifestyle. Forget those unhealthy, unsatisfying, fat-laden quick
alternatives. Choose the healthy option and join the smoothie crowd now. You won't regret it!

1. You may not find *smoothie* in a dictionary. Suggest why.

   ....

   ....

2. Identify the made-up word the author uses to describe how
   tasty smoothies are. ....

3. Underline an example of the rule of three used in this
   extract.

4. In the third paragraph, what effect is created by using
   wonderfully and *magic* to describe smoothies?

   ....

   ....

5. In the final paragraph, which phrases persuade you that
   smoothies are good?

   ....

   ....

   ....

Using antithesis

Find the seven hidden words in the grid by solving the clues below.

All the missing words create antithesis when matched against the clues.

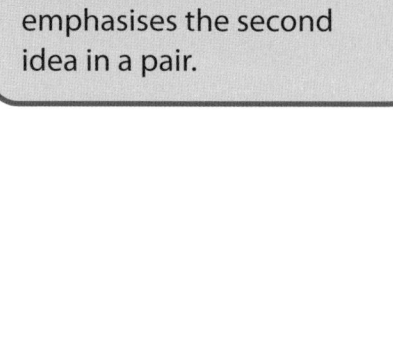

Remember

Antithesis occurs when two contrasting or opposite ideas are used together. It usually emphasises the second idea in a pair.

1. The opposite of healthy is .... (9 letters)

2. If you're not prey you are a .... (8 letters)

3. The opposite of early is .... (4 letters)

4. Yoga is hard work but .... (9 letters)

(**Clue:** It's worth the effort.)

5. Chocolate is delicious but .... (9 letters)

(**Clue:** What effect does it have?)

6. Some dinosaurs were carnivores, others were

.... (10 letters)

U	N	H	E	A	L	T	H	Y	H
C	R	T	A	L	P	I	N	E	F
P	S	E	R	U	T	C	R	T	A
T	R	R	W	H	W	B	H	A	T
O	L	E	C	A	I	L	J	L	T
L	A	M	D	V	R	Q	V	E	E
H	T	K	O	A	N	D	R	N	N
Q	G	R	L	P	T	Y	I	D	I
A	E	S	L	P	H	O	S	N	N
S	R	O	T	A	D	E	R	P	G

Practising emotive language

1. Read the paragraph below. In the relevant columns in the grid, list the reasons readers empathise with the villagers in the passage, then the emotive words used to create this effect. One example of each has been listed for you.

Remember

The purpose of using emotive language is to create an emotional response in the audience.

The river is dry. The fish have died. There is no water to irrigate the precious crops. The very sources that sustain this village have been ruthlessly stolen by the unremitting malevolence of the burning sun. The sun brings life but too much sun brings drought and death. Without water, crops cannot grow, forcing people into malnutrition and starvation.

Reasons	Emotive words used
There is no water	dry

2. Read the paragraph below.

We are Hopeful Springs. With your help, we can bring hope to hundreds of people. With your help, villagers will survive. With your generous giving, you can give fresh water. Villagers *can* flourish even in drought.

a Why does the writer directly address the reader using 'you' and 'your'?

....

....

....

b What is the effect of repeating the phrase 'with your help'?

....

....

....

Lunch is served

Hassan is a blogger and a big fan of cooking but he's a little confused about how to write recipes.

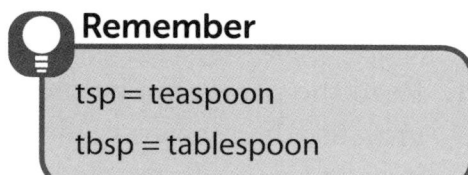

Remember

tsp = teaspoon

tbsp = tablespoon

I really like the bittersweet taste of garlic and lime. Using red and green peppers also gives it colour. Don't add the sauce until the vegetables are cooked properly. It makes 4 servings and takes about 20 minutes to prepare and 10 minutes to cook. You need 250 grams of noodles. To make the sauce you need a tsp of grated lime zest, 2 tbsp of lime juice, 3 tbsp of dark soy sauce and 1 tbsp of brown sugar. You also need 2 cloves of crushed garlic, 3 shitake mushrooms, 1 red and 1 yellow pepper, and 6 cups of thinly sliced green cabbage. You need 2 tsp of cooking oil. Boil the noodles for 2 minutes and drain them. Combine the lime juice, soy sauce, lime zest, brown sugar and garlic in a small bowl. Put to one side. Heat your wok and add 1 tsp of oil. When it's hot, add the mushrooms and peppers. Stir-fry for 2 minutes then add 1 tsp of oil and the cabbage. Stir-fry for about another 2 minutes. Add the sauce and the noodles, toss and serve in bowls.

Organise Hassan's recipe by completing the boxes below.

Servings and preparation time

....

Ingredients (*What's in it?*)

....

....

....

....

....

....

....

....

....

Method (*How to prepare it*)

....

....

....

....

....

....

....

....

....

....

Food for thought quiz

1. What is the main difference between a fact and an opinion?

....

....

2. What is this an example of?

There is nothing difficult about cooking as long as you buy the correct ingredients, measure them accurately and follow the instructions.

....

3. Underline the imperatives in this paragraph:

Jogging isn't for everyone. Visit your doctor before you start and listen to the advice. Buy the correct kind of running shoes and don't sacrifice comfort for fashion. Walk first to warm up then start jogging slowly at a comfortable pace. Make a schedule and keep to it.

4. Complete these sentences using antithesis.

a Fizzy drinks can lead to tooth decay but ....

b .... but too much is dangerous.

5. What is a rhetorical question? Give an example.

....

....

....

....

6. Why is bias important in a piece of persuasive writing?

....

....

....

....

Local holidays

I feel that everyone should appreciate their local area. Nobody should feel they have to leave their country because the grass is greener somewhere else. Some of the places known by local people are the most incredible finds. I remember going to Portugal and finding a very small area with a beach café and behind it there was a little lagoon. People were jumping and diving into the lagoon. It's the same near where I live. There is a run-down castle. So it's not on the tourist trail. I go there lots of times with my friend. But if someone came in from America, for example, they would think, "Oh wow! This is really different."

1. Think about your local area and areas of interest that a tourist might want to see. In the diagram, write six aspects that make it appealing.

2. Write your own blog post to convince tourists why they should visit your local area.

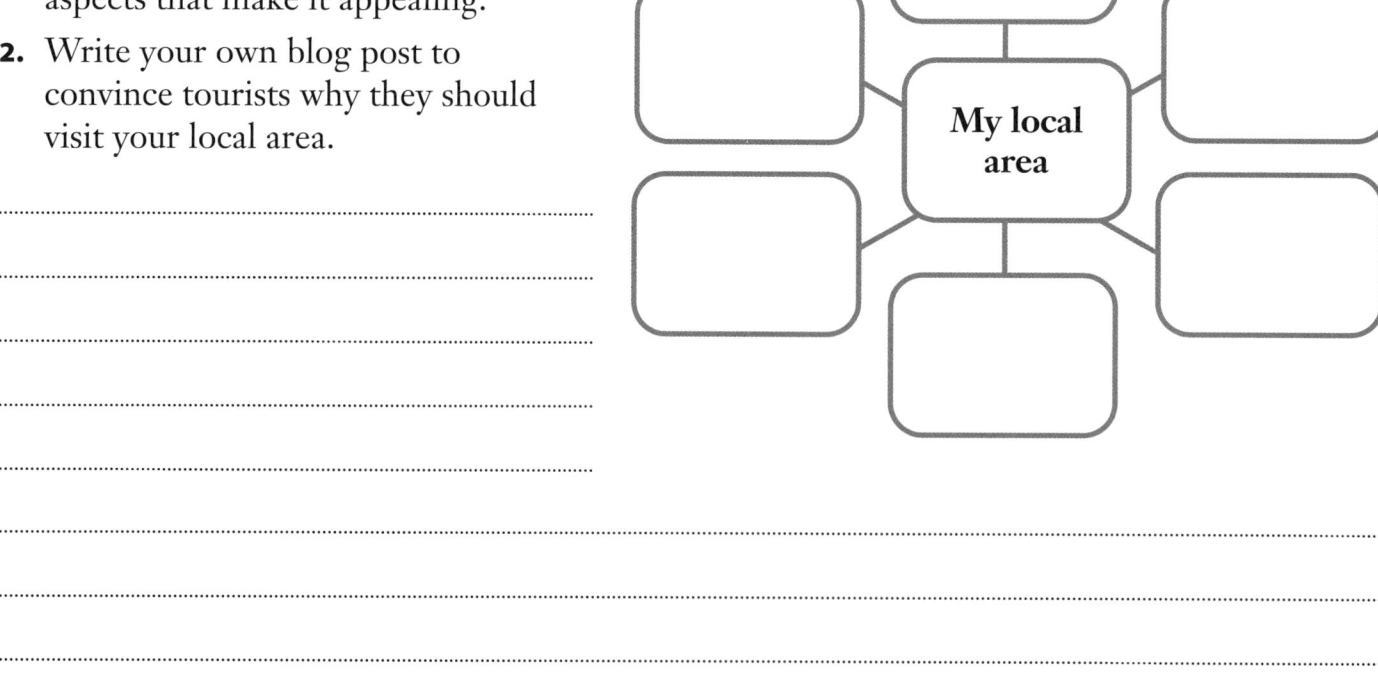

My local area

Practising with context clues

Sometimes there is information around a word that we do not need to work out its meaning. Example:

In 1848, there was not a single kilometre of railway line in India that was functioning.

We do not need the words *kilometre of* as they add nothing to the context.

1. In the sentences below, delete any information not needed for someone to work out what the underlined words mean. Use a dictionary to find definitions for the underlined words.

    a The country's first railway, built by the Great Indian Peninsula Railway (GIPR), was <u>inaugurated</u> in 1853, between Bombay and Thane.

    ....

    b The Allahabad-Jabalpur branch line of the East Indian Railway was opened in June 1867 and was part of a growing <u>network</u> of railway lines.

    ....

    c A man called Brereton was responsible for linking a new shorter line of 600 kilometres, which had to divert around a mountain, resulting in a combined network of 6400 kilometres, which he <u>oversaw</u>.

    ....

    d It became possible to travel on an <u>express</u> train from Bombay to Calcutta. This route was officially opened on 7 March 1870, and the service did not require the train to stop at any of the stations along the way.

    ....

2. Complete the following sentences by adding context clues that would help someone to understand the underlined words. Use a dictionary to find definitions for the underlined words if you need to. The first one has been done for you.

    a The high-speed <u>bullet train</u> from Tokyo .....arrived at the station with the sunlight gleaming on its silvery sides.................

    b The <u>antique</u> steam train had been restored to its original form by ....

    ....

    c When I set off on a long, <u>arduous</u> journey, I ....

    ....

Vowel combinations

Vowels sometimes appear in pairs. When they do, we often hear longer vowel sounds.

1. Find the words listed on the right in the word search.

B	E	L	I	E	V	E	F	D	I	N	G	Y
O	Q	O	L	D	S	X	L	A	K	E	E	P
H	A	L	O	A	T	P	E	U	Z	A	L	L
D	E	W	O	U	A	L	A	G	X	Y	I	U
C	L	A	K	G	I	A	G	H	O	O	R	M
L	H	T	R	H	R	I	U	T	B	U	S	E
E	R	A	E	T	S	N	E	E	A	N	T	E
A	S	T	I	E	V	O	W	R	T	G	W	E
R	U	I	S	R	E	C	E	I	V	E	C	Q
P	I	G	E	O	N	B	M	E	X	N	K	U
G	O	E	S	R	U	M	O	Y	U	P	H	A
O	K	F	R	U	I	T	Z	O	B	I	Z	L
S	O	L	D	I	E	R	B	U	L	N	O	T

BOIL   EQUAL

HEART   LOOK

KEEP   DAUGHTER

EXPLAIN   CLEAR

YOUNG   FRUIT

BELIEVE   PIGEON

GOES   BOUNCE

SOLDIER   LEAGUE

RECEIVE   STAIRS

2. Read the words in the word search aloud. Write down words that do not contain a longer vowel sound, despite containing pairs of vowels.

....

....

3. Identify the words with the following vowel combinations using the definitions provided. Some of the pairs of vowels are at the beginning of the word, some are in the middle.

   a   aa   An anteater found in Africa is an ....

   b   ae   A vehicle that flies in the sky is an ....

   c   ao   The main artery of the body is the ....

   d   ii   A winter sport that requires snow is ....

   e   uu   A space that is entirely without matter is a ....

Writing a news report

Imagine that your journey to school has been disrupted. This could be for any reason you choose. You are a reporter on the scene. Write a report on a separate piece of paper about what you have seen, what has happened and how the situation was resolved.

Examples of how to begin your report:

While standing waiting in line for the school bus to arrive...

Imagine the scene when suddenly a herd of wildebeest...

Aim to write about 150 words. Use the guidelines below.

News reports

When writing a news report, it is important to include the following key features:

1. Headline
Your headline should be a short, eye-catching phrase to grab the reader's attention.

2. Introduction
The introduction should give some information about the story, using facts to state what the news report is about.

3. Main story
You should use the past tense and write in the third person. Include the names of people in the story and refer to them using *he*, *she* or *they*.

4. Facts and opinions
You should state exactly what happens within your news report, but include opinions from witnesses and people affected by the incident to make your story easier to relate to.

5. Quotations
Quotations expressing the opinions of the people you interview can be presented as a feature in your article. This will make these opinions stand out.

6. Photographs with captions
Include photographs with captions to make your news report more interesting.

7. Conclusion
Conclude the news report, giving your own opinion if you wish.

Punctuation – commas and full stops

1. Add commas and full stops to the passage below, taken from *Around the World in 80 Days*, by Jules Verne.

The locomotive whistled vigorously the engineer reversing the steam backed the train for nearly a mile retiring like a jumper in order to take a longer leap then with another whistle he began to move forward the train increased its speed and soon its rapidity became frightful a prolonged screech issued from the locomotive the piston worked up and down twenty strokes to the second they perceived that the whole train rushing on at the rate of a hundred miles an hour hardly bore upon the rails at all. …

It was like a flash no one saw the bridge the train leaped so to speak from one bank to the other and the engineer could not stop it until it had gone five miles beyond the station but scarcely had the train passed the river when the bridge completely ruined fell with a crash into the rapids of Medicine Bow.

2. Read the passage above, pausing at the newly added punctuation.

3. Add to the following user guide for using commas and full stops.

> **Remember**
>
> Remember to use the Language and literacy reference section on pages 76–9 to help you.

Do	Don't
Use commas to slow things down.	Use commas at the end of a sentence.

The birth of the Michelin tyre

The earliest pneumatic tyres had to be glued on with rubber solution. At the end of the 1880s in France, the young owner of a struggling rubber factory, Edouard Michelin, was astounded to learn from a cyclist with a puncture that he had had to wait an entire night for the glue to dry, after he'd repaired the inner tube and re-stuck the casing. Soon after, Edouard introduced a detachable tyre – the 'changeable'. Any cyclist could now repair a puncture, without glue, in fifteen minutes.

From *It's All About the Bike* by Robert Penn

Use the information in the extract above to help you answer the following questions.

1. Which word describes how the owner of the factory felt? What does this word mean? (Use a dictionary to help you.)

....

....

2. Use the context clues in the extract to suggest what the word *detachable* means.

....

....

....

3. In 1880, what did you have to do to fix a puncture?

....

....

....

4. What is different about repairing a puncture now?

....

....

....

Writing challenge

Good descriptive writing uses several features. These include:

- language that sets the scene
- adjectives to give more detail to the objects (nouns)
- adverbs to describe actions but also to give a sense of place, time and circumstances
- use of the senses

- descriptions of the people involved
- descriptions of how main characters felt
- an explanation of how it all ends.

Rewrite the extract below using features of descriptive writing.

We arrived at the boat yard and we found our boat. It was early morning and very windy. The man said we shouldn't risk taking the boat out. We did and we regretted it. The people on the other boat were not too happy at all. The day ended well though.

....

....

....

....

....

....

....

....

....

....

....

....

Joyous journeys quiz

1. Convert the following into a blog entry, writing in the first person.

    The 4.15 p.m. train arrived an hour late. They missed their connecting service.

    ....

    ....

2. Write down six words to describe buildings in which people across the world live.

    ....

    ....

3. Use context clues to suggest the meanings of the following underlined words.

    a   The conditions in the train were <u>sultry</u> so I needed a towel to keep me dry.

        ....

    b   This was <u>uncharted</u> territory for me. It was so exciting to go there.

        ....

    c   I never knew you were <u>aerophobic</u>. Does that mean you're not going to fly to Cairo with us?

        ....

4. Identify the words from the following descriptions. Each one has a vowel sound. Underline the letters that create the sound.

    a   A horse rider puts this on a horse then sits on it. ....

    b   It's the rate at which something moves. ....

    c   On an active holiday people do this on mountains using ropes. ....

5. Add the punctuation you would use in each of these sentences.

    I was frozen it came towards me I panicked I did not enter I wished I'd not ignored that How could it go that fast it was amazing I wondered where it came from

6. Underline the action verbs in the list below.

mountain	run	stop	carriage
explode	shop	jack-knife	stand

This is your life

This is your life

> Drama is about doing and moving, not just reading words on a page.

In your group, decide on a director.

The director tells a story from their own life to the others.

The others then act out the story, supervised by the director.

Afterwards, discuss how good the improvisation was, choose a different director and act out another story.

Keep a list of the stories you act out.

Story 1

....

....

Story 2

....

....

Story 3

....

....

Story 4

....

....

Shakespeare's language

This conversation comes from Shakespeare's play *A Midsummer Night's Dream*. Puck, the servant of Oberon, king of the fairies, has met a fairy who serves Titania, queen of the fairies.

PUCK: How now, spirit! whither wander you?

FAIRY: Over hill, over dale,

Thorough bush, thorough brier,

Over park, over pale,

Thorough flood, thorough fire,

I do wander everywhere,

Swifter than the moon's sphere;

And I serve the fairy queen,

To dew her orbs upon the green.

The cowslips tall her pensioners be:

In their gold coats spots you see;

Those be rubies, fairy favours,

In those freckles live their savours:

I must go seek some dewdrops here

And hang a pearl in every cowslip's ear.

Farewell... I'll be gone:

Our queen and all our elves come here anon.

From *A Midsummer Night's Dream* by William Shakespeare

1. What is different about Shakespeare's language, compared to modern-day English?

....

....

....

2. The fairy tells Puck about where she goes. Name three of the places.

....

....

....

Working with pronouns

You and a friend are the last people to leave a room after meeting two other people. You find a large sum of money on the floor. You have to work out whose money it might be.

Write what you would say to your friend. Include your opinion of whether you should keep the money for yourselves or not. See how many possessive and reflexive pronouns you can include in your writing.

....

....

....

....

....

....

....

Remember

There are four types of pronouns: personal, possessive, reflexive and relative.

....

....

....

....

....

....

....

....

....

....

....

....

Creating characters

How can a character be formed by using suitable adjectives?

1. Read the following extract. Draw the person you imagine in the box.

> When we were kids, we were afraid of the man who lived next door. He always seemed angry, with a surly sneer on his face. He was the sort of person who was always waiting for you to do something wrong. He was spiteful so, when our football went into his garden, he confiscated it and locked it up in his garden shed. "You stupid children!" he'd say.

2. Write a description of the two people below to describe their characters and personalities.

....

....

....

....

....

....

....

....

....

....

A plurality of plurals

The plurals of the ten words on the right are hidden in this word search. Some of them will be unfamiliar to you, so use a dictionary to help you.

Find the plurals and write them below. Next to each one write its singular form. One has been done for you.

BIOGRAPHY
CARIBOU
CARGO
DECOY
NAVY
NEWSFLASH
NOVELTY
PHENOMENON
PIZZA
SENTRY

Q	R	K	R	W	H	D	I	V	U	T	Z	G	W	E	W	H	F	T	B
B	Z	H	T	S	K	O	R	M	S	E	I	T	L	E	V	O	N	G	K
D	K	K	Z	U	G	T	Q	M	N	C	J	L	J	J	T	V	L	V	Y
E	N	T	B	O	V	L	K	I	M	N	B	P	O	L	C	S	D	C	M
S	C	A	R	G	O	E	S	A	N	E	M	O	N	E	H	P	H	N	M
I	E	P	M	F	Z	N	G	P	X	D	V	B	V	M	S	R	E	L	U
D	L	I	O	X	O	D	D	U	P	S	Y	S	A	Z	Z	I	P	O	O
S	O	V	H	S	E	H	S	A	L	F	S	W	E	N	E	J	H	H	H
H	I	Q	N	P	L	I	Z	G	S	E	N	T	R	I	E	S	A	M	S
G	R	N	I	J	A	W	Q	K	C	K	D	O	S	X	Q	E	T	G	C
L	N	D	N	V	P	R	G	Y	F	E	N	D	R	B	N	O	F	Z	L
W	M	T	Q	J	I	S	G	W	C	M	T	H	Q	N	Y	K	J	K	L
Y	U	P	T	P	D	C	K	O	Z	E	N	I	S	L	J	U	B	V	I
S	Z	M	Q	U	J	O	Y	B	I	K	Q	P	E	G	G	B	V	H	H
G	E	G	T	P	V	S	N	K	P	B	A	T	L	U	Q	S	Z	R	Q
B	A	I	L	X	F	R	N	V	V	I	P	M	I	V	O	Q	V	J	V
A	L	Z	V	H	L	J	W	N	X	F	C	A	R	I	B	O	U	K	S
H	A	E	C	A	U	W	H	E	Y	U	H	Z	W	V	T	W	W	B	E
K	D	H	A	I	N	J	T	D	O	D	V	D	M	P	Y	P	M	P	E
H	R	L	X	S	D	S	B	E	B	U	O	T	X	H	M	I	C	R	H

	Singular	**Plural**
1.	sentry	sentries
2.	....	....
3.	....	....
4.	....	....
5.	....	....
6.	....	....
7.	....	....
8.	....	....
9.	....	....
10.	....	....

Word thief

The Bottler used his favourite long words in the Punch and Judy listening playscript on page 96 of the Student Book.

What are your favourite words?

A word thief approaches and steals all the words you know. However, he is kind and lets you keep four words.

1. Write the four words you would like to keep below.

....

....

2. Find five people who have also had their words stolen. Write the shared pool of 20 words down.

....

....

....

3. Use the 24 favourite words you have collected to write a short story or poem. You will need to use articles and connectives to join up the words you have chosen.

....

....

....

....

....

....

....

....

....

....

Stage directions

1. Read the following extract from a play.

2. Add the missing stage directions in the spaces provided.

Your stage directions should set the scene at the beginning, describe how the characters speak, say when they come in and go out, and identify any important movements they make.

Rafa: Where's Sakura?

Laura: [...........................] How do you expect me to know? Really Rafa,

you do annoy me sometimes.

Rafa: [...........................] All right, all right, I only asked. Don't snap at me!

Sakura: [...........................] Hello everybody. What a lovely day! I stopped as

I was coming along just to look at the flowers and listen to the birds.

[...........................] What's the matter? You two look a bit grim. Cheer up!

Rafa: It's Laura. She's snapping everybody's head off. I can't say anything right.

Laura: [...........................] You're horrible! You'll have Sakura ganging up

on me next. I hate you, you are an idiot, Rafa! [...........................]

Rafa: [...........................] For goodness sake, Laura, control yourself. That hurt!

Sakura: There's no need to attack the poor boy. What is the matter

with you?

Laura: [...........................] I hate you all! [...........................]

Sakura: Do you think I should go after her?

Rafa: No, give her time to think things out. She's better off

by herself. Let's go and listen to those birds of yours.

[...........................]

3. Act out the play using your stage directions. Be careful not to make your play physically violent.

Dating the drama quiz

1. Where in the theatre are you if you are:

   a in the wings?

   ....

   b upstage?

   ....

   c downstage?

   ....

   d in the auditorium?

   ....

2. a Explain how you can be a 'bag of nerves'.

   ....

   b What do actors mean by the phrase 'break a leg'?

   ....

3. Pretend you have to go for an interview. Which one of these words describes the way you would speak?

miserably   *confidently*   *pompously*

Explain your answer.

....

....

4. Suggest what Sonya means when she says "boredom and idleness are infectious" in *Uncle Vanya*. Do you agree with this statement?

....

....

5. In a play, what is meant by:

   a the setting?

   ....

   b the characters?

   ....

   ....

Exploring genre

Genres are different kinds of literature that have features specific to the themes and ideas included. So a story that belongs to the science fiction genre may include:

aliens   faraway planets   time travel

spaceships   advanced technology.

Fit these plots from different genres into the most appropriate bubbles:

a Boy and girl meet and fall in love

b Cowboy hero saves town

c Master criminal steals jewels

d Spies chase scientific formula

e Dragon threatens kingdom

f Princess saves elves from troll

g Secret agent exposes spy network

h Girl breaks up with boyfriend

i Police inspector chases thieves

j Gunfighters meet in duel

Remember

Sometimes themes and ideas overlap between genres so a story about a man and a woman falling in love can belong to both romance and fantasy if, for example, it is set in a magical kingdom threatened by dragons and other mythical creatures.

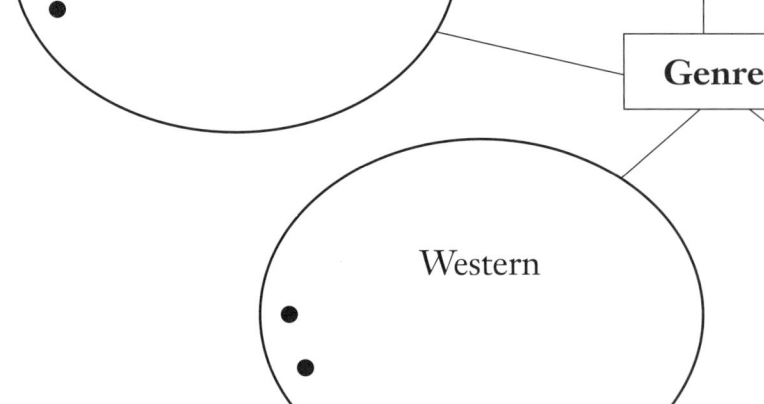
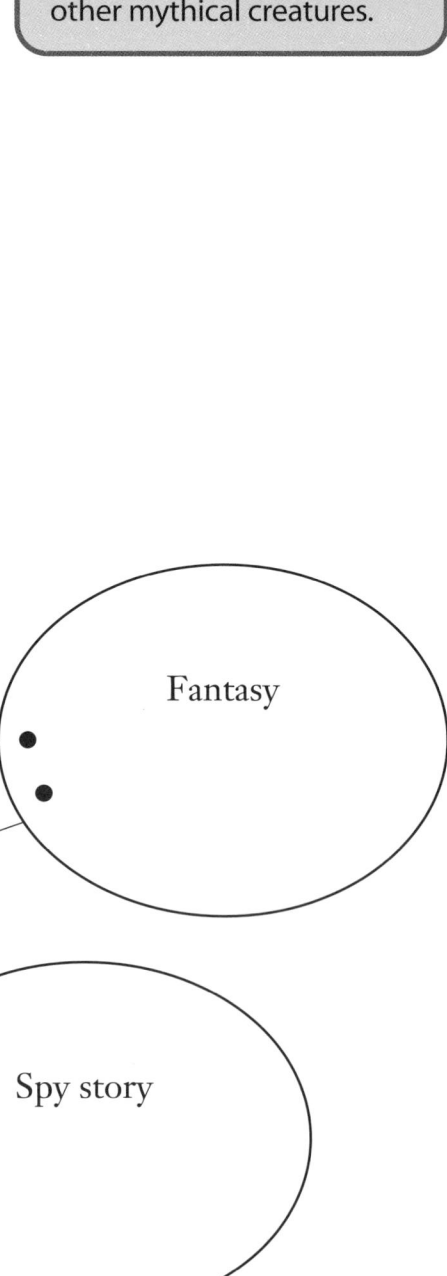

Engaging your imagination

Read this extract from the discussion between Amin, Deepak and Hikari.

Hikari: In the future you won't have to travel anywhere. All your school lessons will be transmitted to you over a super-fast hypernet that will mean you can study from home with a teacher who is thousands of miles away. You'll feel like you're in a classroom with other students from all over the world but it will all be virtual reality created by your computer at home.

Deepak: That'd be my kind of school but I wouldn't be sitting in a virtual reality classroom. I'd be learning about other planets in Science whilst pretending to stand on the surface of Mars or sitting at the bottom of the ocean with my pet dolphin and learning about marine biology.

Amin: That would be cruel, Deepak. You can't turn wild animals into pets!

Deepak: Hold that thought, my friend. I'm only joking about the dolphin.

1. What do you think of Hikari's ideas? Do you think they are possible in the future? Give two reasons for your answer.

....

....

....

....

2. If you had the choice, where would you most like to study in a virtual reality world? Explain your answer.

....

....

....

....

3. What would be your choice of pet if you could have anything you wanted, real or imaginary? Why?

....

....

Using contractions

Contractions shorten words to make them quicker and easier to say. They use apostrophes to show where the letters have been missed out.

Remember

Contractions are used in informal situations and not formal writing.

1. Change these words into their contracted forms:

    a Cannot ....

    b It is ....

    c I am ....

    d Shall not ....

    e You will ....

2. Change these contracted words into their more formal forms:

    a I've ....

    b That'd ....

    c We're ....

    d I'll ....

    e Won't ....

3. Deepak is writing an important letter. He wants to study Marine Biology at university, but he has used too many contractions. Underline his 12 mistakes. Then write his letter out again more formally on a separate piece of paper.

I'm so happy I can't wait to study Marine Biology at your university. I've loved dolphins all my life. They're so cute and friendly. It's my dream to work with them. I couldn't imagine a better career. I shan't sleep until I've received your reply so I hope you'll accept me. Please don't say you've no places left on the course as that'll be a big disappointment for me.

Understanding ideas

Charlotte, the main character in *In the Nick of Time*, has travelled back in time to 1952. Instead of being excited by her adventure, she is frightened and wants to return to the present day.

1. Imagine you have travelled back to 1952. Would you be excited? Would you want to go home? Would you feel a mixture of feelings? List reasons for and against your journey on the watches below.

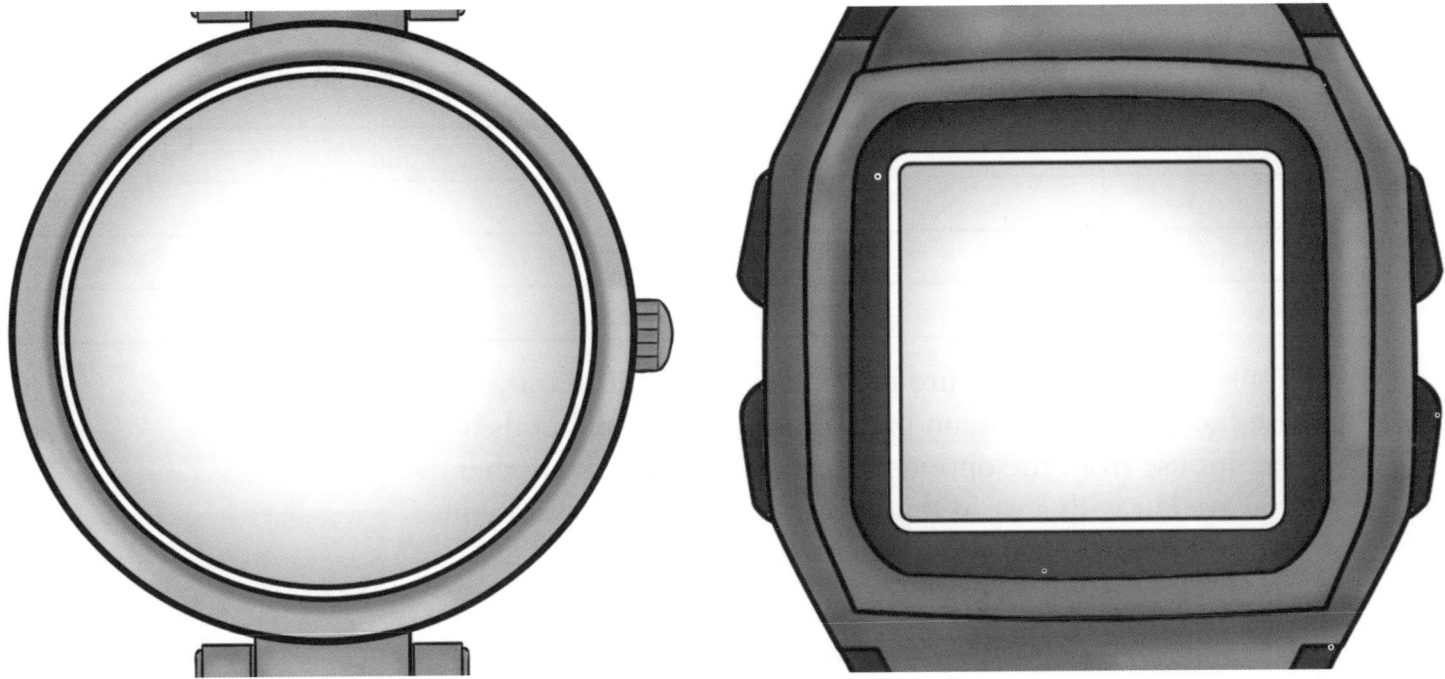

2. If you travelled in time, when and where would you most like to go? Who would you most like to meet?

When? ....

Where? ....

Who? ....

Why? ....

....

3. On a large sheet of paper, design your own machine to travel through time. Label it to describe the most important parts.

Using prefixes

1. Write each word below beside the prefix in the grid that changes its meaning.

correct legal worn sense spelling agree tie possible polite lock understanding precise capable logical interested fiction stop appropriate literate adventure contented perfect deed fair

Remember

Prefixes are letters added to the front of a word to change its meaning.

Prefix	Words
dis	
il	
im	
in	
mis	
non	
un	

2. Your rocket is ready to fire but it needs fuel. It can only use fuel pods that contain prefixes. Delete the fuel pods it cannot use from the options below. (Hint: Check whether you are left with a word that means the opposite when you remove the first two or three letters.)

unnecessary   disguise   image

misbehave   unsolved   important

innocent   illness   mistimed

unloved

Alliteration and adjectives

1. Look at the example of alliteration (right). Write an explanation of what alliteration is.

   ....

2. The underlined words below are adjectives.

   The monster opened its <u>huge</u> jaws and gave a scream that was both <u>terrible</u> and <u>ear-splitting</u>.

   Write an explanation of what an adjective is.

   ....

3. Advertisements often use both alliteration and adjectives. Imagine that a new museum about the future of science and technology is opening. Write a leaflet advertising the museum. Remember to use plenty of adjectives and alliteration.

   Here is an opening to get you started.

   Are you interested in the awesome and amazing world of science – and all the terrific opportunities technology can offer us? If so, head straight to the magnificent Museum of Science and Technology – it's a brilliant day out for everyone!

Super sizzling science fiction!

....

....

....

....

....

....

....

....

....

Planning short stories

Read this description of a science fiction novel.

In the year 2120, the scientific field of robotics has become so advanced that robots that look and act like humans are integrated into normal society. They perform duties thought too unimportant or dangerous for human citizens to do, like manual labour and fighting fires. They are ideal servants as they do not need to eat or sleep and they do not require payment for their services. Everyone is pleased with this arrangement until one dramatic night when one of the robots is accused of committing a terrible crime and everything changes...

To plan a successful short story it is useful to think of your ideas as a jigsaw puzzle.

Complete each piece using the description above.

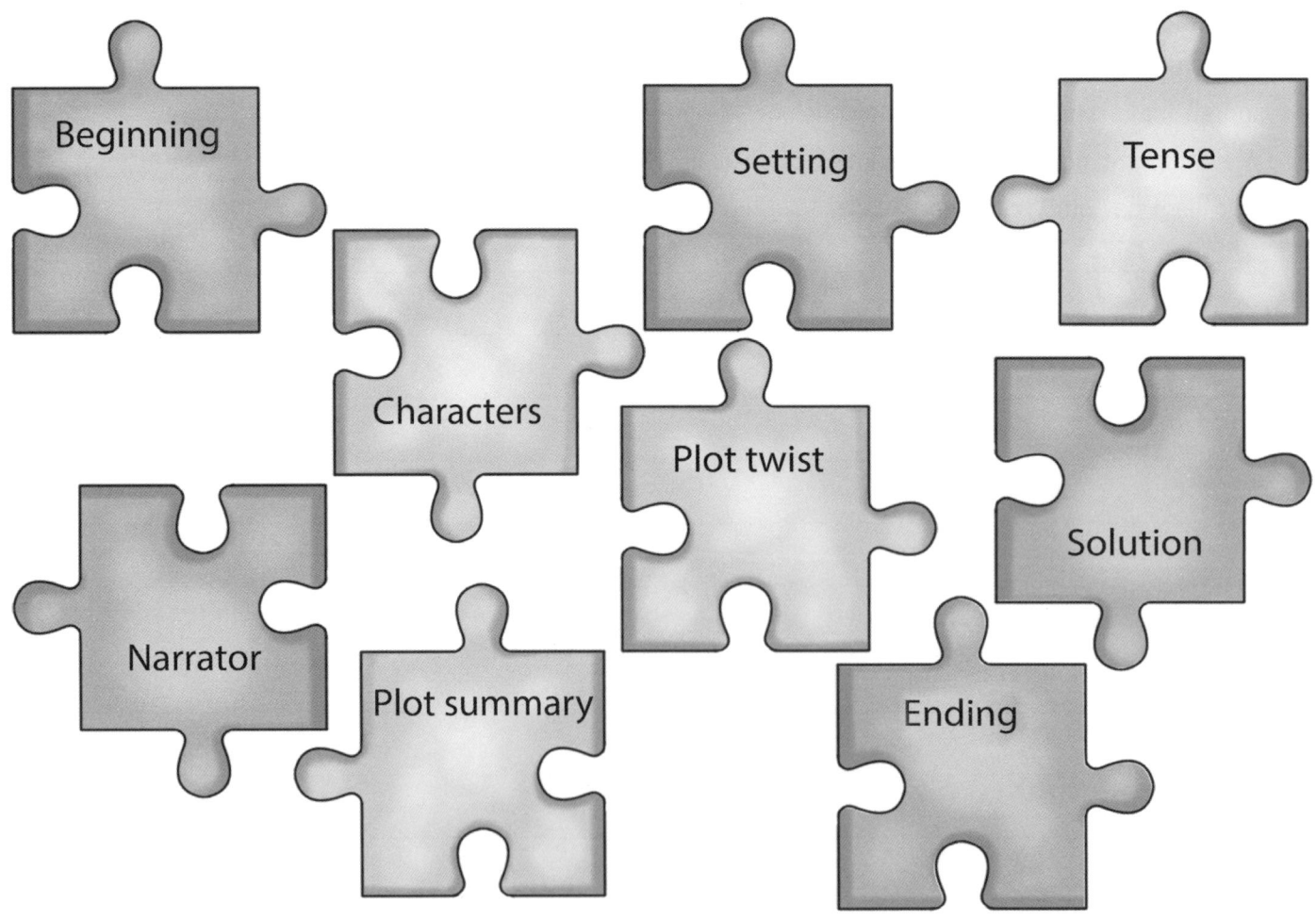

Beginning
Setting
Tense
Characters
Plot twist
Solution
Narrator
Plot summary
Ending

Sizzling science quiz

1. When is it acceptable to use contractions?

....

....

2. Write a sentence including the contracted forms of *will not* and *cannot*.

....

....

3. Whats wrong with this sentence? Write the correct version below.

....

4. What happens to the meaning of a word when you join the prefix *un* to it?

....

5. Name three other prefixes that perform the same task as *un-*. Give an example for each one.

....

....

....

6. What is alliteration and why is it used?

....

....

7. Write an example of an alliteration.

....

....

8. Put the different parts of the jigsaw on page 58 in order from start to finish.

....

....

....

Hairy history

Timelines

It's hard to understand time. If 20 students aged 12 years stood in a long line, their ages added together would be 240 years.

1. Complete the timeline for your life so far. Fill in the boxes to say what was happening to you and your family at those times.

You may need to talk to your family to complete this task.

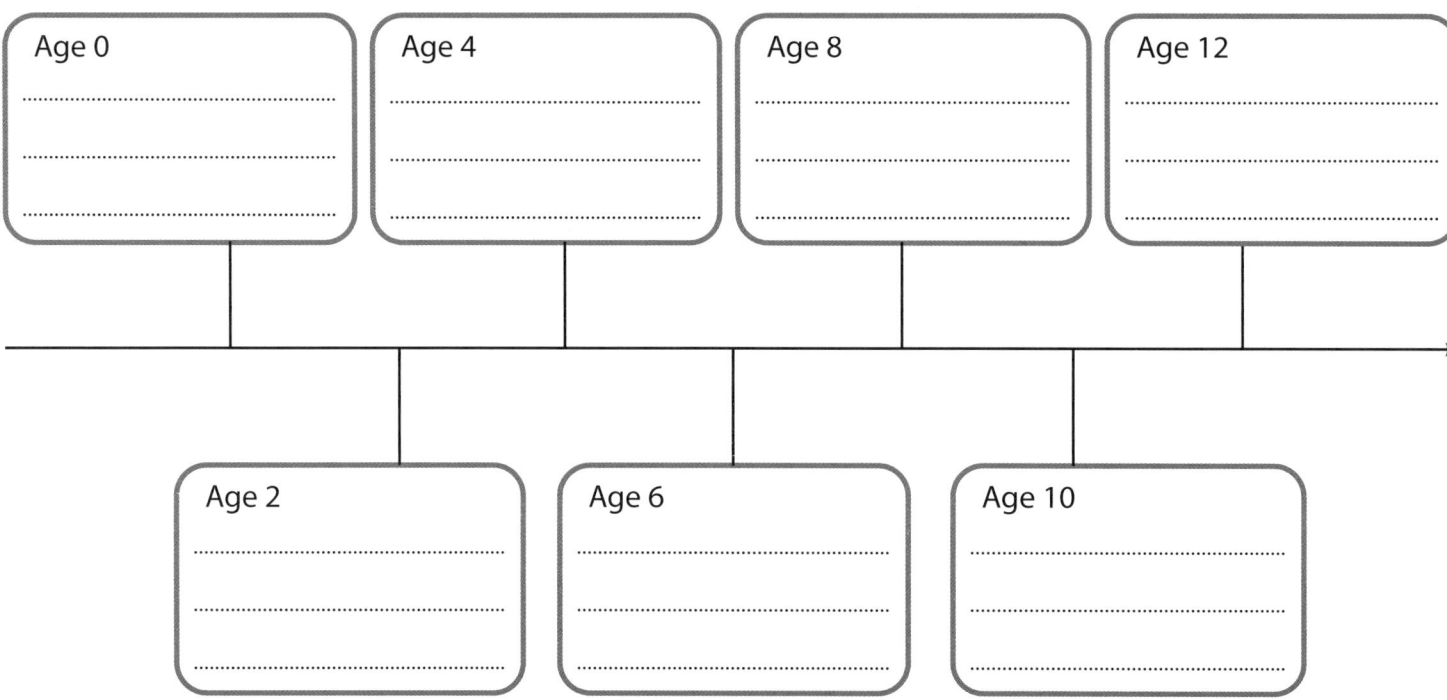

| Age 0 | Age 4 | Age 8 | Age 12 |

| Age 2 | Age 6 | Age 10 |

2. Research and draw a similar timeline to the one above for your country. Use the time period 1750–2000.

   Use books or the Internet to help you.

Memories of school

Read these memories of Andrei's schooldays from 60 years ago.

When I was at the boys' school we'd always start with assembly, standing in lines for twenty minutes. In winter we'd come out of the freezing cold with fingers like blocks of ice; in summer, we'd sweat with the heat. Winter was worse. We'd stand outside at break and drink a bottle of milk through a straw. If anyone was seen blowing bubbles, he'd be going to the Headmaster. Sometimes the milk was frozen, so we couldn't drink it. If the playing fields were frozen, we'd put on running shorts and shirts and set off on a six-kilometre, cross-country run along the river and up the hills. At the top you could see the sea, but we were too busy running through the farmyard, avoiding savage animals that used to chase us. If we didn't keep running we'd freeze, we'd be late back to school and miss the buses to our villages. Sometimes, it was almost dark when we trundled in through the school gates. Indoor games was warmer, but it was dangerous. I was scared that I would fall off the narrow, wooden beam set high above the floor that we had to tiptoe across.

Answer the following questions.

1. How does Andrei describe the following?

   a Assembly: ....

   b How the boys drank their milk: ....

   c The view at the top of the hills: ....

   d How the boys went home: ....

2. Did Andrei like his school? Use words from the extract to explain your answer.

   ....

   ....

   ....

3. Compare Andrei's school with your own. What are some of the similarities and differences?

   ....

   ....

   ....

Using commas

1. Read the sentences below. Then add commas to the sentences. How have the commas changed the meaning of the sentences?

"I'm important!"

"Let's eat Daddy."

"We're going to learn to paint kids."

"Slow children at play."

"I love cooking my Mum and my two cats."

"Be careful of barbecuing horses and children when on the beach."

"At the hospital she found Dad and Mum and Baby David lying in a little cot."

> ### Remember
>
> Some common uses of commas:
>
> - to separate words in a simple list of three or more items
> - to separate two adjectives when they are interchangeable
> - when using a word such as *however* to begin a sentence
> - on either side of someone's name if he or she is being spoken to
> - to introduce, or interrupt, direct quotations
> - when using clauses that begin with *and*.

2. Read the following and add commas where needed.

   a Maria had just arrived home from work and was eating her lunch when she heard her brother Georgi shout down from upstairs.

   b "Please and as quick as you can fetch me my book Maria. It's on the kitchen table."

   c "I can see several books here Georgi" answered Maria. "Which one do you mean? Is it the dusty old one?"

   d "I want the green modern mathematics book" said Georgi "and I need it now."

   e However Georgi would have to wait. Maria as it was her lunch break would finish off her coffee biscuits yoghurt and a few grapes before attending to her brother's needs.

   f "I want it" added Georgi "because it has my homework notes in it."

Word builder

1. Complete this crossword using the clues provided.

Across

2 Time to be free

4 It is what you expect

5 Left behind

6 An antonym of *boring*

8 Full of something nasty

Down

1 To interest deeply

3 Total change of government

7 The action of putting money in for profit

2. Make your own mini-crossword – two clues across and two clues down. Use the words below.

HISTORIC   DIFFERENT   RUGGED   PLANTATIONS

Contractions

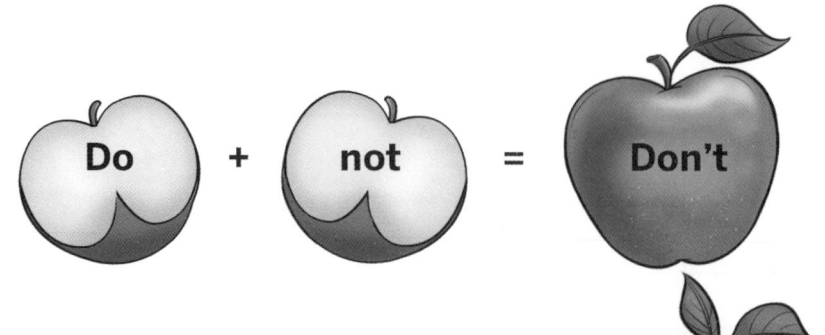

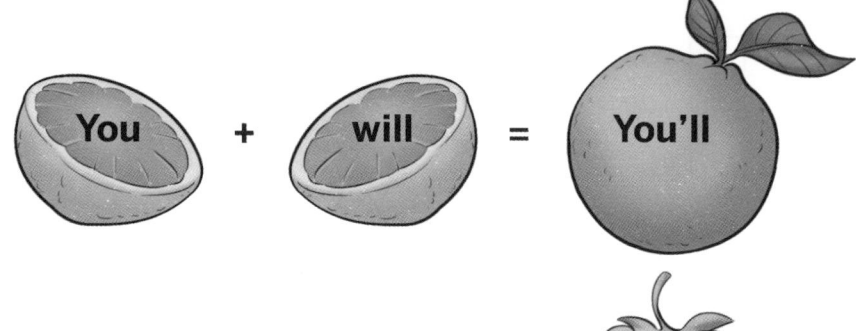

Remember

The apostrophe in contractions replaces one or more letters in the original words.

1. Identify the words in these contractions.

    a couldn't ....   **c** there's ....

    b he'll ....   **d** would've ....

2. Write the contractions for these phrases.

    a Aisha is ....   **c** they have ....

    b will not ....   **d** Adnan will ....

3. Pretend you are annoyed with your friend, brother or sister. Write a short paragraph of what you may say. Try to use at least five contractions in your writing.

....

....

....

....

Past, present and future

1. Make notes on how you think your life is different to your grandparents' lives when they were children, 50 years ago, using the subjects in the boxes below.

Power supply

....

....

....

Transport

....

....

....

Communication

....

....

....

Hobbies

....

....

....

2. How do you think our world will be different in 50 years' time? Think about driverless cars, drones delivering parcels, holidays in space and schools that are run by computers.

   Write your ideas in the spider diagram. Use one box for each idea.

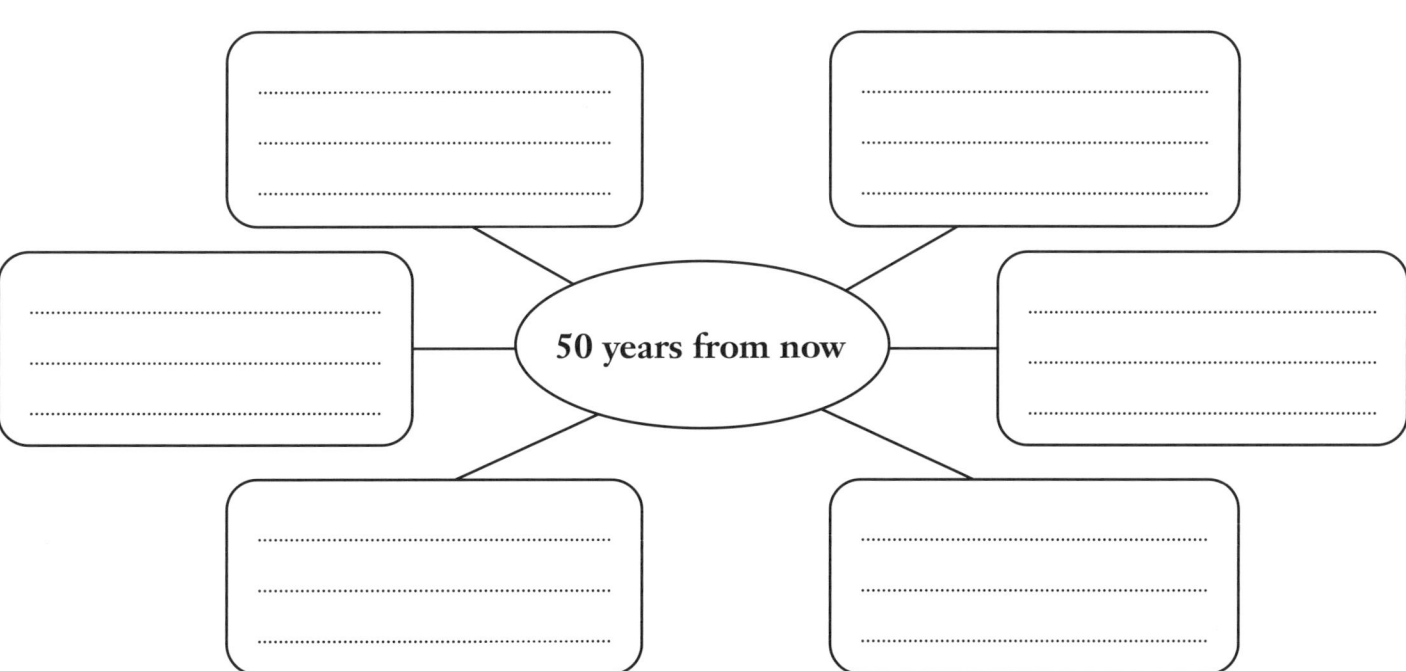

Autobiographies

Write a section of your autobiography. Here are some ideas for you to think about.

Remember

A biography tells you about someone's life history. An autobiography is about your own history.

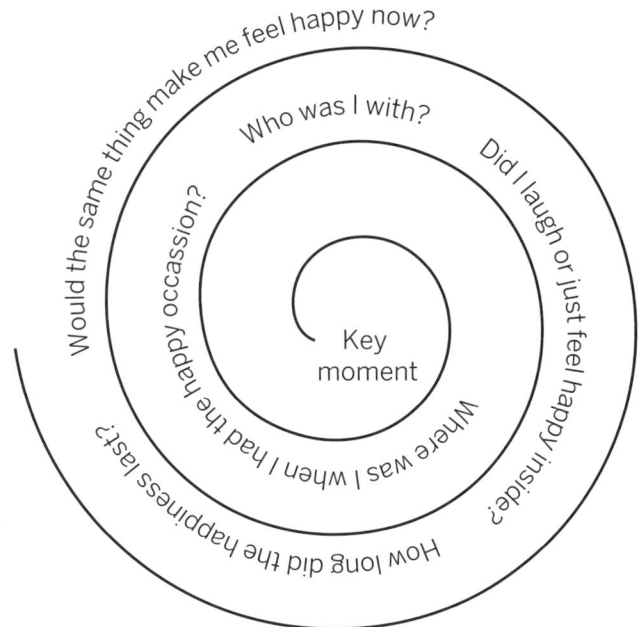

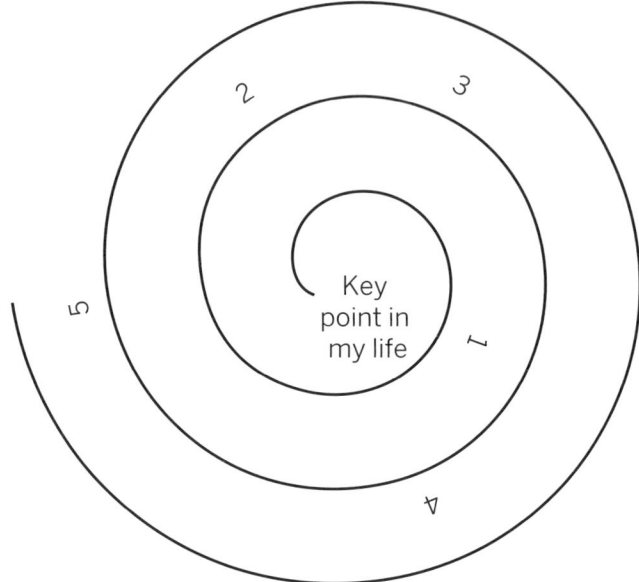

Each spiral is like a journey along a timeline, with key moments along the way.

Fill out a copy of the blank spiral by following these steps:

1. Think of a key moment in your life. It could be a memory of a specific event or location.

2. At the centre of your spiral, write a few words to describe it.

3. As the spiral widens, it forms your journey from your key moment to the present. Write notes along the spiral explaining how you got to where you are today.

4. Add more words and sentences on a different page to explain fully and link the stages together. You should then have a part of your autobiography.

5. Add more spiral journeys, converted to paragraphs.

Hairy history quiz

1. Give the definition of *historian*, *historic* and *prehistoric*.
Then write a sentence in which you use all three words.

Historian: ....

Historic: ....

Prehistoric: ....

My sentence: ....

....

2. What would be a good:

a synonym for *crumbling*? ....

b antonym for *repetitive*? ....

3. Choose the correct option. If I wanted to link simple
sentences together, I would use:

a a coordinating sentence   **c** a coordinating conjunction

b a coordinating comma   **d** a word such as *they*, *your* or *his*.

4. Write a sentence including three contractions. Then write
it again without contractions.

....

....

....

....

5. Write in the missing words.

A dictionary is where I would .... words, but
if I wanted to find a word with a similar meaning, I would
look in a ....

6. 'Happy birthday, Alana.' This is a good example of a
sentence. True or false? ....

7. When you make a contraction, such as 'What's the time?',
what does the apostrophe tell you?

  ◯ A question mark is needed.   ◯ There is a plural.

  ◯ One or more letters are missing.   ◯ Two words have been shortened.

Writing – a poem is a painting that speaks

1. Look at the detail of these ancient woodcuts. Write down what you see. What do you imagine when you look at them?

....

....

....

....

2. Read the opening lines of poems about the two woodcuts. How would you complete the poems? Try to add to them here.

   a Behind the towers and tall turrets, a lonely prisoner lies

   ....

   ....

   b Is this tough skin
   Or is it metal armour
   I am in?

   ....

   ....

Spelling beetle

Lament for a Dead Cow is all about an animal.

The names of different animals are listed below. Play a game to practise your spelling of these words.

Find a friend or a family member to help you. If they cannot help, practise your spelling by using the *look, cover, write, check* method.

Easy words	More difficult words	Hardest words
bear	chimpanzee	aardvark
bull	crocodile	alpaca
fly	dolphin	bonobo
hamster	elephant	hippopotamus
horse	gazelle	llama
monkey	gerbil	lynx
rabbit	giraffe	mosquito
shark	leopard	penguin
snail	reindeer	rhinoceros
tiger	whale	wildebeest

Your finished beetle could look like this!

Ask your helper to pick one word at a time – they should vary the difficulty of words they ask with each round. Each time you spell a word correctly, draw an item on your beetle body – first a head, then 2 feelers, 2 eyes, carapace and 6 legs (12 items in all).

Here are some beetle bodies to get you started:

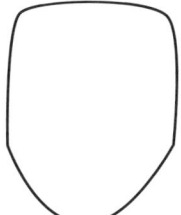

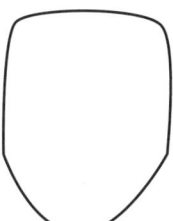

Making comparisons

Imagine that you need to buy beds for your two younger siblings. You've looked at many different beds and these are the three you like – but you can't make up your mind.

Remember

When making comparisons, you look for similarities and differences.

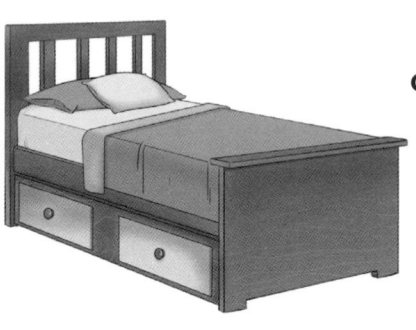

or

Think of the needs of your siblings and write a comparison of the two options.

I like the idea of buying the two single beds because ....

....

....

....

I'm also attracted by the idea of buying a bunk bed because ....

....

....

....

I've finally made up my mind to buy the .... because

....

....

....

Speech marks and exclamation marks

Speech marks (" and ") can be used to show direct speech.
They are also called inverted commas.

1. The first two lines in the extract below have all their
    punctuation marks. After that, the speech marks are
    missing.

    Fill in the missing punctuation.

    "What did you do at school today, Ahmad?" asked his father.

    "Nothing much," answered Ahmad. "Our usual teacher was away."

    Let's see, said his father with a sigh. It says on your timetable that you

    had science and English lessons today as well as Arabic.

    Oh, we did stuff, mumbled Ahmad. Lots of stuff.

    This won't do! said his father sharply. What a forgetful boy you are!

    Now tell me immediately what you did in the English lesson!

> **Remember**
>
> Remember to add
> punctuation to the end of
> a person's speech, *before*
> closing the speech marks.

2. Continue the conversation by writing what Ahmed said
    next and how his father replied.

    ....

    ....

    ....

3. Did you notice the exclamation marks (!) in the passage?
    Exclamation marks are used when someone speaks loudly,
    suddenly or angrily.

    Copy out the following sentences, adding exclamation
    marks in the appropriate places.

    a "Don't be so rude"

    ....

    b "What a funny thing to say"

    ....

    c "How clever you are"

    ....

    d "Mind that car. It nearly ran you over"

    ....

Prose and poetry

Thomas Hood lived in the 19th century, in a place where November was a dark and cold month. The following extract from his poem describes how miserable he feels.

From 'November'

No sun – no moon!

No morn – no noon!

No dawn – no dusk – no proper time of day –

No sky – no earthly view –

No distance looking blue –

No road – no street – no "t'other side the way" –

No end to any **Row** –

No indications where the **Crescents** go –

No top to any steeple –

No recognitions of familiar people –

No warmth, no cheerfulness, no healthful ease,

No comfortable feel in any member –

No shade, no shine, no butterflies, no bees,

No fruits, no flowers, no leaves, no birds –

November!

Thomas Hood

Glossary

Crescent a curved street of houses

Row a name given to some streets that have lines of houses

1. Read the poem aloud. What tone of voice will you use?

2. Write four ways in which the poem is different from prose.

....

....

....

....

3. Write three sentences in prose to summarise this extract.

....

....

....

Crazy poems

Preena enjoys reading nonsense poems. These poems don't necessarily make you laugh, some of them are simply silly. One of Preena's poems was about a man with a beard. It was a type called a limerick.

Before reading limericks, practise this rhythm several times.

Di di-di-di di-di-di da

1. Read the two poems below, applying different rhythms to each.

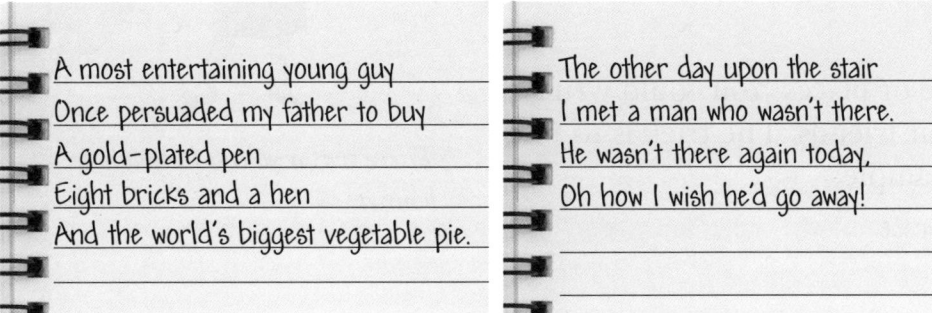

A most entertaining young guy
Once persuaded my father to buy
A gold-plated pen
Eight bricks and a hen
And the world's biggest vegetable pie.

The other day upon the stair
I met a man who wasn't there.
He wasn't there again today,
Oh how I wish he'd go away!

There was an old man with a beard

2. Read the poems again. In the box below each poem, write down or draw what you imagine as you read.

Writing your own limerick

Limericks contain five lines.

Lines 3 and 4 are shorter than lines 1, 2 and 5.

Lines 1, 2 and 5 have one rhyme and lines 3 and 4 have another rhyme. Example:

> Di di-di-di di-di-di da R1
>
> Di di-di-di di-di-di da R1
>
> Di di-di-di dum R2
>
> Di di-di-di-dum R2
>
> Di di di-di-di di-di-di da R1

There was a young lady whose bonnet...

Some limericks are about people or places. You could write one about yourself or one of your friends. The trick is to find rhymes to go with the name. Example:

> There once was a student called Grace
>
> Who had a most wonderful face

You might tell a little story, for example, 'I went for a walk in the park'. Be careful when choosing the last word in the first line – make sure that you will be able to find fun rhymes for it.

The nonsense is most likely to be in the last three lines.

Write two limericks in the space below.

....

....

....

....

....

....

....

....

....

Nurturing nature quiz

1. In Tennyson's poem, the eagle fell 'like a thunderbolt'. Suggest why Tennyson did not simply say that the eagle fell 'very quickly'.

....

....

2. **a** In 'Ozymandias', Shelley wrote *trunkless*, *lifeless* and *boundless*. What does *–less* on the end of a word mean?

....

b Now add *–less* to *care*, *thought* and *fear*. Write a sentence using each of your new words.

Care ....: ....

Thought ....: ....

Fear ....: ....

c Now try adding *–ness* and *–ly* to each of your new words and write them below.

....

....

3. Informal language is often used in conversation.

a Give an example of informal language.

....

b Would you expect to use informal language when talking to your teacher? Explain your answer.

....

....

4. **a** Narrative poems tell a story.

Narration means: ....

Narrator means: ....

b Use the stem from the words in part **a** to identify the verb meaning 'to tell a story'.

Verb: ....

Language and literacy reference

Active voice versus passive voice – Verbs are active when the subject of the sentence (the agent) does the action. Example: *The shark swallowed the fish*. Active verbs are used more in informal speech or writing.

Verbs are passive when the subject of the sentence has the action done to it. Example: *The fish was swallowed by the shark*. Passive verbs are used in more formal writing such as reports. Examples: *An eye-witness was interviewed by the police. Results have been analysed by the sales team.*

Sometimes turning an active sentence to passive, or vice versa, simply means moving the agent:

- The shark (agent and subject) + verb = active
- The fish (object) + verb = passive

Adjective – An adjective describes a noun or adds to its meaning. They are usually found in front of a noun. Example: *Green emeralds and glittering diamonds*. Adjectives can also come after a verb. Examples: *It was big. They looked hungry*. Sometimes you can use two adjectives together. Example: *tall and handsome*. This is called an adjectival phrase.

Adjectives can be used to describe degrees of intensity. To make a comparative adjective you usually add *–er* (or use more). Examples: *quicker; more beautiful*. To make a superlative you add *–est* (or use most). Examples: *quickest; most beautiful*.

Adverb – An adverb adds further meaning to a verb. Many are formed by adding *-ly* to an adjective. Example: *slow/slowly*. They often come next to the verb in a sentence. Adverbs can tell the reader: how – *quickly, stupidly, amazingly*; where – *there, here, everywhere*; when – *yesterday, today, now*; how often – *occasionally, often*.

Adverbial phrase – The part of a sentence that tells the reader when, where or how something happens is called an adverbial phrase. It is a group of words that functions as an adverb.

Examples: *I'm going to the dentist **tomorrow morning*** (when). *The teacher spoke to us **as if he was in** a bad mood* (how); *Sam ran **all the way home*** (where). These adverbials are called adverbials of time, manner and place.

Alliteration – Alliteration occurs when two or more nearby words start with the same sound. Example: *A slow, sad, sorrowful song.*

Antecedent – An antecedent is the person or thing that a pronoun refers back to. Example: *President Alkira realised that his life was in danger.* 'President Alkira' is the antecedent here.

Antonym – An antonym is a word or phrase that means the opposite of another word or phrase in the same language. Example: *shut* is an antonym of *open*. Synonyms and antonyms can be used to add variation and depth to your writing.

Audience – The readers of a text and/or the people for whom the author is writing; the term can also apply to those who watch a film or to television viewers.

Clause – A clause is a group of words that contains a subject and a verb. Example: *I ran*. In this clause, *I* is the subject and *ran* is the verb.

Cliché – An expression, idiom or phrase that has been repeated so often it has lost its significance.

Colloquial language – Informal, everyday speech as used in conversation; it may include slang expressions. Not appropriate in written reports, essays or exams.

Colon – A colon is a punctuation mark (:) used to indicate that an example, explanation or list is being used by the writer within the sentence. Examples: *You will need: a notebook, a pencil, a notepad and a ruler. I am quick at running: as fast as a cheetah.*

Conditional tense – This tense is used to talk about something that might happen. Conditionals are sometimes called 'if' clauses. They can be used to talk about imaginary situations or possible real-life scenarios. Examples: *If it gets any colder the river will freeze. If I had a million pounds I would buy a zoo.*

Conjugate – To change the tense or subject of a verb.

Conjunction – A conjunction is a word used to link clauses within a sentence such as: *and, but, so, until, when, as*. Example: *He had a book in his hand when he stood up.*

Connectives – A connective is a word or a phrase that links clauses or sentences. Connectives can be conjunctions. Examples: *but, when, because*. Connectives can also be connecting adverbs. Examples: *then, therefore, finally.*

Continuous tense – This tense is used to tell you that something is continuing to happen. Example: *I am watching football.*

Discourse markers – Words and phrases such as *on the other hand, to sum up, however* and *therefore* are called discourse markers because they mark stages along an argument. Using them will make your paragraphs clearer and more orderly.

Exclamation – An exclamation shows someone's feelings about something. Example: *What a pity!*

Exclamation mark – An exclamation mark makes a phrase or a short sentence stand out. You usually use it in phrases like 'How silly I am!' and more freely in dialogue when people are speaking. Don't use it at the end of a long, factual sentence and don't use it too often.

Idiom – An idiom is a colourful expression which has become fixed in the language. It is a phrase which has a meaning that cannot be worked out from the meanings of the words in it. Examples: *'in hot water' means 'in trouble';* It's *raining cats and dogs.*

Imagery – A picture in words, often using a metaphor or simile (figurative language) which describes something in detail: writers use visual, aural (auditory) or tactile imagery to convey

how something looks, sounds or feels in all forms of writing, not just fiction or poetry. Imagery helps the reader to feel like they are actually there.

Irregular verb – An irregular verb does not follow the standard grammatical rules. Each has to be learned as it does not follow any pattern. For example, *catch* becomes *caught* in the past tense, not *catched.*

Metaphor – A metaphor is a figure of speech in which one thing is actually said to be the other. Example: *This man is a lion in battle.*

Non-restrictive clause – A non-restrictive clause provides additional information about a noun. They can be taken away from the sentence and it will still make sense. They are separated from the rest of the sentence by commas (or brackets). Example: *The principal, who liked order, was shocked and angry.*

Onomatopoeia – Words that imitate sounds, sensations or textures. Examples: *bang, crash, prickly, squishy.*

Paragraph – A group of sentences (minimum of two, except in modern fiction) linked by a single idea or subject. Each paragraph should contain a topic sentence. Paragraphs should be planned, linked and organised to lead up to a conclusion in most forms of writing.

Parenthetical phrase – A parenthetical phrase is a phrase that has been added into a sentence which is already complete, to provide additional information. It is usually separated from other clauses using a pair of commas, dashes or brackets (parentheses). Examples: *The leading goal scorer at the 2014 World Cup – James Rodriguez, playing for Columbia – scored five goals. The leading actor in the film, Hollywood great Gene Kelly, is captivating.*

Passive voice – See active voice.

Person (first, second or third) – The first person is used to talk about oneself – *I/we*. The second person is used to address the person who is listening or reading – *you*. The third person is used to refer to someone else – *he, she, it, they*.

- *I feel like I've been here for days.* (first person)
- *Look what you get when you join the club.* (second person)
- *He says it takes real courage.* (third person)

Personification – Personification can work at two levels: it can give an animal the characteristics of a human and it can give an abstract thing the characteristics of a human or an animal. Example: *I was looking Death in the face.*

Prefix – A prefix is an element placed at the beginning of a word to modify its meaning. Prefixes include: *dis-, un-, im-, in-, il-, ir-*. Examples: *impossible, inconvenient, irresponsible*.

Preposition – A preposition is a word that indicates place (*on, in*), direction (*over, beyond*) or time (*during, on*) among others.

Pronoun – A pronoun is a word that can replace a noun, often to avoid repetition. Example: *I put the book on the table. It was next to the plant.* 'It' refers back to the book in first sentence.

- Subject pronouns act as the subject of the sentence: *I, you, he, she, it*.
- Object pronouns act as the object of the sentence: *me, you, him, her, it, us, you, them*.
- Possessive pronouns show that something belongs to someone: *mine, yours, his, hers, its, ours, yours, theirs*.
- Demonstrative pronouns refer to things: *this, that, those, these*.

Questions – There are different types of questions.

- Closed questions – This type of question can be answered with a single-word response, can be answered with 'yes' or 'no', can be answered by choosing from a list of possible answers and identifies a piece of specific information.

- Open questions – This type of question cannot be answered with a single-word response; it requires a more thoughtful answer than just 'yes' or 'no'.

- Leading questions – This type of question suggests what answer should be given. Example: *Why are robot servants bad for humans?* This suggests to the responder that robots are bad as the question is "why are they bad?" rather than "do you think they are bad?" Also called loaded questions.

- Rhetorical question – Rhetorical questions are questions that do not require an answer but serve to give the speaker an excuse to explain his/her views. Rhetorical questions should be avoided in formal writing and essays. Example: *Who wouldn't want to go on holiday?*

Register – The appropriate style and tone of language chosen for a specific purpose and/or audience. When speaking to your friends and family you use an informal register whereas you use a more formal tone if talking to someone older, in a position of authority or who you do not know very well. Examples: *I'm going to do up the new place.* (informal) *I am planning to decorate my new flat.* (more formal)

Regular verb – A regular verb follows the rules when conjugated (e.g. by adding *–ed* in the past tense, such as *walk* which becomes *walked*).

Relative clause – Relative clauses are a type of subordinate clause. They describe or explain something that has just been mentioned using *who, whose, which, where, whom, that* or *when*. Example: *The girl who was standing next to the counter was carrying a small dog.*

Relative pronoun – A relative pronoun does what it says – it takes an idea and relates it to a person or a thing. Be careful to use *who* for people and *which* for things. Examples: *I talked to your teacher, who told me about your unfinished homework. This is my favourite photo, which shows you the beach and the palm trees.*

Restrictive clause – Restrictive clauses identify the person or thing that is being referred to and are vital to the meaning of the sentence. They are not separated from the rest of the sentence by a comma. With restrictive clauses, you can often drop the relative pronoun. Example: *The letter [that] I wrote yesterday was lost.*

Semi-colon – A semi-colon is a punctuation mark (;) that separates two main clauses. It is stronger than a comma but not as strong as a full stop. Each clause could form a sentence by itself. Example: *I like cheese; it is delicious.*

Sentence – A sentence is a group of words that expresses a complete thought. All sentences begin with a capital letter and end with a full stop, question mark or exclamation mark.

- Simple sentences are made up of one clause. Example: *I am hungry.*

- Complex sentences are made up of one main clause and one, or more, subordinate clauses. A subordinate clause cannot stand on its own and relies on the main clause. Example: *When I joined the drama club, I did not know that it was going to be so much fun.*

- Compound sentences are made up of two or more main clauses, usually joined by a conjunction. Example: *I am hungry and I am thirsty.*

Good writers use sentences of different lengths to vary the pace of their writing. Short sentences can make a strong impact while longer sentences can make text flow.

Simile – A simile is a figure of speech in which two things are compared using the linking words *like* or *as*. Example: *In battle, he was as brave as a lion.*

Simple past tense – This tense is used to tell you that something happened in the past. Only one verb is required. Example: *I wore a hat.*

Simple present tense – This tense is used to tell you that something is happening now. Only one verb is required. Example: *I wear a hat.*

Standard English – Standard English is the form of English used in most writing and by educated speakers. It can be spoken with any accent. There are many slight differences between Standard English and local ways of speaking. Example: *We were robbed* is Standard English but in speech some people say, *We was robbed.*

Suffix – A suffix is an element placed at the end of a word to modify its meaning. Suffixes include: *-ible, -able, -ful, -less.* Examples: *useful, useless, meaningful, meaningless.*

Summary – A summary is a record of the main points of something you have read, seen or heard. Keep to the point and keep it short. Use your own words to make everything clear.

Synonym – A synonym is a word or phrase that means nearly the same as another word or phrase in the same language. Example: *shut* is a synonym of *close*. Synonyms and antonyms can be used to add variation and depth to your writing.

Syntax – The study of how words are organised in a sentence.

Tense – A tense is a verb form that shows whether events happen in the past, present or the future.

- *The Pyramids are on the west bank of the River Nile.* (present tense)

- *They were built as enormous tombs.* (past tense)

- *They will stand for centuries to come.* (future tense)

Most verbs change their spelling by adding *–ed* to form the past tense. Example: *walk/walked.* Some have irregular spellings. Example: *catch/caught.*

Topic sentence – The key sentence of a paragraph that contains the principal idea or subject being discussed.

Word cloud dictionary

Word and definition	Notes

Ache *noun*
A dull, continuous pain.

Agriculturalist *noun*
A farmer.

Ancient *adjective*
Belonging to the distant past, very old.

Archaic *adjective*
Belonging to former or ancient times.

Auditorium *noun*
The part of a theatre or hall where the audience sits.

Bark *noun*
The outer covering of a tree's branches or trunk.

Beheld *verb*
Saw something.

Blue *adjective*
A colour.

Break *verb*
To divide something into pieces.

Bright *adjective*
Shining; giving a strong light.

Bulging *adjective*
Swelling or protruding outwards in a curve.

Burger *noun*
Piece of beef formed into a flat round shape, eaten grilled.

Burning *adjective*
Being on fire.

Burst *verb*
To break something apart suddenly or violently.

By heart
To learn something in such a way that you can repeat it from memory.

Calisthenics *noun*
Physical exercise done with little or no apparatus.

Captive *adjective*
Taken prisoner.

Word and definition   **Notes**

Cardio-vascular *adjective*
Relating to the heart and blood vessels.

Cast *noun*
Performers in a play or film.

Chaos *noun*
Great disorder.

Choke *verb*
To cause someone to stop breathing properly.

Clamp *verb*
To fix something firmly.

Cliff-hanger *noun*
A tense and exciting ending to an episode of a story.

Clothe *verb*
To put clothes on someone or something.

Clung
From the verb *to cling*, held on tightly.

Cognitive *adjective*
Relating to the mental process of perception, memory, judgement
and reasoning, as contrasted with emotional and volitional processes.

Cola *noun*
A brown carbonated drink.

Colossal *adjective*
Extremely large; enormous.

Combine *verb*
To join or mix together.

Conflagration *noun*
A large, destructive fire.

Congealed *adjective*
A liquid which has become jelly-like.

Core strength *noun*
The strength of the underlying muscles of the torso.

Cramped *adjective*
Not having enough space.

Cruel *adjective*
Causing suffering or pain.

Crumbling *adjective*
Broken into small fragments or crumbs.

Word and definition	Notes
Decay *noun* The process or result of going bad or rotten.	
Desolate *adjective* Sad and lonely	
Desperate *adjective* Extremely serious or hopeless; reckless and ready to do anything.	
Diverse *adjective* Of several different kinds; varied.	
Downstage *adjective* Near the audience, close to the front of the playing area.	
Drain *verb* To take water away through a pipe or ditch.	
Drench *verb* To wet something all through.	
Emaciated *adjective* Very thin from illness or starvation.	
Excruciating *adjective* Extremely painful.	
Exhilarating *adjective* Making a person feel very happy and excited.	
Extraordinary *adjective* Very unusual.	
Extraterrestrial *adjective* From beyond earth's atmosphere; from outer space.	
Fertile *adjective* Producing good crops / offspring / ideas.	
Flash *noun* A sudden bright light.	
Flexibility *noun* The ability to change or adapt, bend or stretch without breaking.	
Flicker *verb* To shine or burn unsteadily.	
Forthwith *adverb* Immediately.	
Fringe *verb* To hang as a decorative edging.	

Word and definition	Notes
Frown *verb* To wrinkle the forehead in worry or anger.	
Froze *verb* To turn into ice, feeling extremely cold.	
Futuristic *adjective* Very modern as though belonging to the future.	
Ghostly *adjective* Like the spirit of a dead person appearing in this world.	
Gigantic *adjective* Extremely large; huge.	
Gleam *noun* A bright shine.	
Glint *noun* A brief flash of light.	
Glittering *adjective* Shining with little flashes of light.	
Grandiose *adjective* Trying to seem large and impressive.	
Growl *verb* To make a deep angry sound in the throat.	
Half-hearted *adjective* Not very keen or enthusiastic.	
Haunted *adjective* Visited by a ghost or often visiting a place.	
Hiss *verb* To make a sound like an s.	
Historian *noun* A person who studies history.	
Historic *adjective* Famous or important in history.	
Historical *adjective* To do with history.	
Hoarse *adjective* Having a rough or croaking voice.	
Holistic *adjective* The treatment of the whole person.	

Word and definition	Notes
Honorary *adjective* Given as an honour.	....
Horrify *verb* To make someone feel very afraid or disgusted.	....
Hug *verb* To clasp closely in your arms.	....
Humane *adjective* Kind-hearted.	....
Hypertension *noun* Abnormally high blood pressure, a state of great psychological stress.	....
Implore *verb* To beg someone to do something.	....
Inadequate *adjective* Not enough, not good enough.	....
Incorrigibly *adverb* Incapable of being reformed or changed.	....
Inferno *noun* A raging fire.	....
Inhabit *verb* To live in a place.	....
Inhale *verb* Breathe in.	....
Irritably *adverb* Annoyed, bad-tempered manner.	....
Jack-knifed *adjective* Folded against itself.	....
Jerk *verb* To make a sudden, sharp movement.	....
Kaleidoscope *noun* A place or thing full of colour or variety.	....
Large *adjective* Big.	....
Lash *verb* To hit with a whip or a stick.	....
Loop *verb* To form something into a loop; encircle.	....

Word and definition	Notes

Magnificent *adjective*
Grand or splendid.

Make fun of *verb*
To tease, laugh at or joke about.

Meagre *adjective*
Scanty in amount, barely enough.

Miserably *adverb*
Unhappily.

Monstrosity *noun*
A monstrous thing.

Murder-suspense whodunit *noun*
A psychological thriller story.

Natural *adjective*
Done or produced by nature; not by humans or machines.

Nifty *adjective*
Skilful or effective.

Nippy *adjective*
Quick or nimble.

Ornamentation *noun*
The decoration of a place with beautiful things.

Peak *noun*
The highest or most intense part of something.

Pedestal *noun*
A raised base upon which a statue etc. stands.

Perch *verb*
To sit on the edge of something high or narrow.

Perish *adverb*
To die or be destroyed.

Pompously *adverb*
Excessively grand and self-important.

Pop *noun*
A fizzy drink.

Pour *verb*
To flow; rain heavily.

Precious *adjective*
Very valuable, greatly loved.

Word and definition	Notes

Prehistoric *adjective*
Belonging to a time before written records of events were made.

Producer *noun*
The organiser of the performance of a play or the making of a film.

Prominent *adjective*
Important; well-known.

Prompter *noun*
A person who reminds an actor or speaker of words when they have forgotten them.

Propel *verb*
To push something forward.

Put you off *verb*
To dissuade or discourage someone.

Pyrotechnics *noun*
A fireworks display.

Quaint *adjective*
Attractively old-fashioned or odd.

Racing *adjective*
Moving or going very fast.

Rainbow *noun*
An arch of all the colours of the spectrum formed in the sky when the sun shines through the rain.

Refrain *verb*
To stop yourself from doing something or the chorus of a song.

Refrigerate *verb*
To make food or drink extremely cold in order to preserve and keep it fresh.

Repetitive *adjective*
Full of repetitions.

Reproachfully *adverb*
Upset and disappointed by something someone has done.

Respiratory *adjective*
The process of breathing.

Reward *noun*
Something given in return for a good deed or an achievement or success.

Word and definition

Notes

Robotics *noun*
The study of the design, construction and use of robots.

Sarcastically *adverb*
With irony or cutting remarks to express disapproval or contempt.

Scalp *verb*
To cut or tear the scalp from a person or animal.

Scoff *verb*
To eat something completely or greedily.

Scorching *adjective*
Very hot.

Scratchy *adjective*
If something is scratchy it irritates the skin.

Sculptor *noun*
A person who makes sculptures.

Serve *verb*
To give out food to people at a meal.

Shine *verb*
To give out or reflect light.

Shredded *adjective*
Cut into small pieces.

Sling *noun*
Loop or band placed around something, e.g. a broken arm, to support or lift it.

Snake *verb*
To move with a winding or twisting motion.

Sneer *verb*
To speak in a scornful way.

Sob *verb*
To cry.

Solemnly *adverb*
Not smiling or cheerful.

Sparkling *adjective*
Shining with tiny flashes of light.

Spectacular *adjective*
Impressive or striking.

Word and definition   **Notes**

Speed of light *noun*
The distance light can travel in a unit of time.

Sponge *verb*
To wipe or wash something with a sponge.

Spotlight *noun*
A strong light that can shine on one small area.

Stagnant *adjective*
Not flowing.

Sturdy *adjective*
Strong and vigorous or solid.

Sugar cane *noun*
The plant from which sugar is obtained.

Summit *noun*
The top of a mountain or hill.

Sunbaked *adjective*
Baked or dried out due to exposure to the sun's heat.

Sunburnt *adjective*
Burned by the sun, causing discoloured surface.

Swanky *adjective*
Shown off in a conceited or boastful way.

Taut *adjective*
Stretched tightly.

That's tough
An expression used to sympathise with someone who has had
bad news or experienced something bad.

Thirsty *adjective*
Wanting or needing to drink.

Time travel *noun*
Travel through time into the past or the future.

Toast *verb*
To heat the surface of something to make it brown and crisp.

Torrential *adjective*
Rain that pours down violently.

Toss *verb*
To throw something, especially up into the air.

Tragedy *noun*
A very sad or distressing event.